Contents

Acknowledgements

Foreword

The Story Behind 'Geocaching GPS'

What is Geocaching?

Stories of Romance

A Beach Proposal

Found It!

Operation Treasure Hunt

Caching on One Leg

Making the Kansas Heartland Geocaches

A Surprising Tradition(al) Cache

Stories of Adventure

Geocaching in Prison

Who Says Smoking Kills?

Our First FTF or A Fool-hearty Twilight Quest

Another Name For Fun

Lake Mary's Curse

An Adventure In Retail

Midspring's Night Dream

Lewis Hills Geocaching Event

Bobbing for Bob

A Real Cliff Hanger

Concert on a Waterfall

On a Stormy Day

Good Lock

Hot Adventure on Hot Wheels

The Challenging Geocache

Steel Fears

Cache-22

Stories of Connection

Ode to Swamp Rats

A Quick Stop Along the Way

Beauty in Abandonment

Thanks For The Cache

Buckskin Run's Last Geocache

An Obsession is Born

How Geocaching Changed a Life

Walk With Me

Finding Friends

How "Penguinmolly" Became "GeopenguinsH"

Along for the Hike

Inspiration from "The Greats"

Geocaching is for Lovers

Extras

Common Geocaching Terms

Getting Started Geocaching

A Favor to Ask…

About the Editor

Other Books From Kimberly Eldredge

Acknowledgements

Special thanks to Mr. Bryan Roth from Geocaching.com for not only his tireless work to make sure this game runs smoothly and is fun for all, but also for his generous gift of time to write the foreword. Mr. Roth, your contribution makes this a much better book.

I'd also like to thank the 43 wonderful geocachers in the book – without you and your families this book never would have happened. I appreciate all you do to place caches, support each other, and the time and effort you put into your story. I'm so proud of you all and honored to be your editor and a geocacher in your company.

And, as always, thanks for their support and tireless "cheerleader" effort goes to my folks, Bruce and Rose Eldredge, and my soul-mate, Ben. Here's to many happy years for geocaching for us all!

Foreword

If you ask geocachers how they would describe the game of geocaching, almost all of them would include the phrase 'treasure hunting' in their description. They would generally be using the word 'treasure' to describe one or more of the millions of physical boxes hidden around the world waiting to be found by geocachers.

If you look a little bit deeper, however, you would find that the other treasures they've found have a value that greatly exceeds physical boxes. In fact, all over the world, geocachers are finding and experiencing the type of treasures that make life truly worth living. These treasures are the adventures they share and the relationships they create with other people along the way.

At its core, geocaching is a game of hide and seek played by many millions of people all over the world. Among all these people worldwide, there are different cultures, different traditions and different beliefs. Yet, when it comes to geocaching, they are all bound together by a spirit of adventure, a yearning to explore, and a desire to create, share, and play together. It is, in part, this common bond that makes the creation of lasting relationships among geocachers so prevalent within the community.

Geocachers are putting their time and effort into creating many different ways for others to have fun, including geocaches, events, trackables, and more. Families with children, students, business travelers, retirees, scout troops, and everyone else can easily find and experience outdoor adventures, just about anywhere in the world.

Through geocaching, many geocachers have met their life-partner, explored far off destinations, formed international friendships, achieved positive fitness results, faced fears, conquered adversity, reconnected with family members, given back to their communities, and much more. Their stories, treasures in themselves, are then shared at events, online, on the trail, and in books like this one.

Over the past 15 years as one of three co-founders of Geocaching.com, I have been honored to witness geocaching touching the lives of millions of people worldwide in so many positive ways. Aside from geocaching being a large part of my occupation over the past 14 years, geocaching has had a profound effect on my personal life.

On November 18, 2001, I was invited to attend the Washington Potluck and Quilting Bee Geocaching Event (GC26D6) at Marymoor Park in Washington State by my friend and co-founder Jeremy Irish. It was the first geocaching event that I had ever attended and it changed the course of my life forever.

When geocachers meet other geocachers at events or on the trail, conversations flow easily. We already have so much in common and we can always talk about the game and our experiences. Of course, there is often something fun to find nearby. This lends itself to the easy creation of new connections, impromptu geocaching excursions, and even chance meetings with our future spouses. Such was the case with me.

It was at this potluck geocaching event that I met a wonderful geocacher named Heidi and her son Dylan. We met, talked about geocaching, went on a few geocaching dates, and fell in love. After getting married and legally adopting Dylan, Heidi and I had a baby boy named Nicholas. Over the past many years, we have been fortunate to enjoy many wonderful geocaching excursions together. We've attended geocaching events together, and met geocachers from all over the world, spending time with them and developing true friendships. We have shared adventures with people that we never would have met if not for geocaching. And now, we consider these geocachers to be part of our extended family. For me, the relationships that we have with other geocachers are the very best part of this game.

I believe that many geocachers have experienced something similar, developing friendships, sharing adventures, and establishing strong bonds with those who they've met through geocaching whether in person or online. It is people inspiring other people to get outside and have fun. It is people joining others on the trail and at events. Geocaching is touching lives because it is creating opportunities for people to play together and build relationships.

So, to all of you who create geocaches, all of you who host geocaching events, and all of you who contribute positively to the global geocaching community in any way, thank you! You are helping to build community and make connections among people all over the world.

Enjoy these stories. Then, go outside, have some adventures and make some new friends. Treasures abound!

– Bryan Roth,

Geocaching Co-Founder

Geocaching name: Bryan

The Story Behind 'Geocaching GPS'

I've been geocaching for a long time – like since 2008. I've run a geocaching blog at FindYourGeocache.com since 2009. Something that has always struck me is the wonderful stories geocachers have. Sure, there's the "There's great swag in this cache" or the "Muggles were EVERYWHERE around that cache" type stories, but there were even more stories of how a game of "Using multi-million dollar safelights to find Tupperware® in the woods" has changed lives.

My life's purpose it to help people write and publish their books – so what better use of my gifts and talent than to do the same for the geocaching community?

The stories in this book were collected via a free writing contest. My goal was to bring you 30 stories and this book has 43. Authors and stories come from four different continents: North America, Europe, Africa, and Australia and a multitude of countries. The wonderful response to this project from the geocaching community completely blew my mind! I know many geocachers and muggles alike who are thrilled to be finally holding this book in their hands.

For many of the authors, this is their first publication. The thing they call have in common, however, is that they all have an amazing feel-good story to share.

Most of the authors included in this anthology are not professional authors. Their stories have been lightly edited for clarity, but the words are their own. For a few of the authors, English is NOT their first language so the story was edited for clarity but also to leave the voice intact. The unusual turns of phrase or awkwardness is intentional to make sure their personality comes through!

I'm honored to have been entrusted with their words, their stories, and their messages. I hope you enjoy reading "Geocaching GPS" as much as we all enjoyed creating it for you.

Kim Eldredge

Kim Eldredge

TippySheep

Note: Under the story's title, you'll find both the real name of the author and their geocaching name.

There may be terms you don't recognize, like Muggle or GZ, that are unique to the game of geocaching. Please find an explanation of these terms at the end of the book. Additional information about geocaching can be found in the "Extras" section.

What is Geocaching?

Just in case you've never heard of this game or received this book as a gift!

Geocaching is a high-tech treasure hunting game played throughout the world by adventure seekers equipped with GPS devices. The basic idea is to locate hidden containers, called "geocaches" or just simply "caches", and then share your experiences online.

Other geocachers obtain the coordinates and seek out the cache using their handheld GPS devices. The finding geocachers record their find in the logbook and then they also record the find online.

Geocaching is enjoyed by people from all age groups, with a strong sense of community and support for the environment.

Geocache Containers

A geocaching container should be water-proof, critter-proof, and well hidden. It can be anything from a micro-cache to a container large enough for "swag". Geocache container sizes range from film canisters often called "microcaches," too small to hold anything more than a tiny paper log, to five-gallon buckets or even larger containers.

Geocache containers are often camouflaged with paint or tape to make them blend in with their surroundings. Imagine finding a film canister, spray-painted green and brown, in a forest! With a GPS to help, that is exactly what geocachers do every day.

For the traditional geocache, a geocacher will hide a waterproof container, containing a log book (with pen or pencil) and trinkets or some sort of treasures, then note the cache's coordinates. These coordinates, along with other details of the location, are posted on the Geocaching.com website.

Geocache Prizes or "Swag

"Swag" are the goodies left inside a geocache. The rule is: take something of equal value to what you are leaving. You don't have to take anything if you're more into the thrill of the find.

Typical cache treasures are not high in monetary value but may hold personal value to the finder. Aside from the logbook, common cache contents are unusual coins or currency, small toys, ornamental buttons, geocoins, or other small items

Occasionally, higher value items are included in geocaches, normally reserved for the first to find, or "FTF", or in locations which are harder to reach.

Speaking of "FTF", geocachers use a type of "shorthand" to make notes to other geocachers in the logbook. Examples are: TNLN (Took Nothing, Left Nothing); SL (Signed Log); and TFTF (Thanks For The Find.)

Trackable Items

Attach a Travel Bug tag to an item, create a mission for its travels, and then place the item into a geocache. As your Travel Bug moves from geocache to geocache, picking up stories and photos along the way, you can live vicariously through the bug's adventures!

Cachers who initially place a Travel Bug or Geocoin often assign specific goals for their trackable items. One such goal could be to pass it westward across the continent.

Geocoins work similarly to Travel Bugs in that they are trackable and can travel the world. Some geocoins are often created as signature items by geocachers and can also be used as collectibles. Collectable geocoins are not trackable.

Stories of Romance

A Beach Proposal

Duane Bolin

El Pollo Loco Gang

Karen and I met on a lovely October weekend during the Fall Festival in Evansville, Indiana. During our first few months of dating, I shared with her many "war stories" of my geocaching exploits in the past. We both love the great outdoors and had gone hiking together several times so it was only a matter of time before we decided to begin geocaching together.

Karen and I knew we were meant to be together from the moment we met. Nevertheless, we took things slowly. We enjoyed many adventures together over the next year. In addition to hikes in the Hoosier National Forest, we explored all sorts of interesting places during our travels.

In particular, we had a blast exploring Chicago, Illinois as only geocachers can!

As time passed, I knew I wanted to ask Karen to marry me… but I wanted it to be a memorable surprise. With a trip to Florida approaching, I decided that a walk on a deserted beach would be the perfect way to pop the question. But where could I find the perfect location?

As has happened so many times in the past, I found what I wanted through geocaching. As I planned our Florida trip, I kept my eyes open for interesting caches and locations. It wasn't long before all the pieces began to fall into place.

I awoke on March 25, 2014, in Bradenton, Florida. I had butterflies in my stomach, because I was so excited to get going. I told Karen that we would be going geocaching the whole day, seeing a variety of sights and ending the day with a nice hike.

We headed south toward the first cache of the day, a difficult puzzle that presented the opportunity for a first-to-find three years in the making. The cache was called Evil Angel (GC2NFTW) and it certainly lived up to its name. Hidden in February 2011, the cache had remained unsolved and unfound for three years.

When I first saw the puzzle, the cipher text looked familiar. As it turns out, I had solved a similar puzzle in Indiana, so I knew which website to use. Unfortunately, I didn't know the exact code to use to extract the solution, so I had to finish the code-cracking by hand. Eventually I was able to crack the puzzle.

I was excited when we reached ground zero, as I had never had the chance to solve a puzzle and get a first-to-find on an infamous puzzle that had sat unfound for multiple years. Karen and I searched for a few minutes with no luck. I was afraid our special day was going to get off to a bad start. Could we really come this far with the correct coordinates and still not make the find?

Nope! After walking a few feet away from ground zero, I turned and spotted the cache. Relief swept through me, and we opened the cache to find a blank log. Success! We signed in as the first-to-find, took a few pictures, and then headed toward the coast.

Our next stop was Sanibel Island. We visited the virtual cache at the old lighthouse (GC919C) and then checked out a couple of cool EarthCaches on the beaches nearby. Karen wanted to linger a bit longer, but I told her better things were ahead. So we headed north toward Venice.

After enjoying some delicious gelato in downtown Venice, we headed toward our promised hike and destination cache: Casperson's Beach Cache (GC4CEF). I chose this cache because of the first lines of its description: "An easygoing 1.5 mile trek along the Florida Gulf of Mexico shoreline. You can take the inland trail to the cache and then walk along the beach on the way back."

The cache description promised an interesting hike with chances to see authentic Florida wildlife, followed by a stroll along a mostly-deserted stretch of pristine beach. It did not disappoint. Along the hike to the cache, we saw blooming cacti, beautiful birds, several gopher tortoises, and even an armadillo!

After playing with a couple of the tortoises and taking some turtle "selfies," we made our way to ground zero. Karen came up with the find on the cache, and we signed the log. At that point, we were ready for some beach time. Little did Karen know that the best was yet to come.

We made our way toward the shore through an area that was a bit like a jungle. When we spied the Gulf, we realized that we were on a small bluff above the shore. We found a tree whose roots made a series of steps down to the sand.

Nearby, we found a palm tree that stretched from the sand up to the top of the small bluff. It was the perfect spot to sit and take in the sun and waves. I sat down on the trunk of the tree and motioned for Karen to join me. She sat down and leaned back against me. I wrapped my arms around her and kissed the back of her neck.

A gentle breeze brought the sounds of sea gulls to our ears. The clouds that had blanketed the sky earlier in the day had finally departed. The sunshine warmed our skin, and we could taste the salt in the dewy air. We dug our toes down into the soft, yet rough sand, soaking up the beauty of this lonely stretch of beach.

I wanted to let that moment play out forever, but the anticipation that had been building within me all day would not wait any longer. I pulled my Bible out of my pack and told Karen I wanted to share a verse with her. She seemed a little surprised, so I thought she might be getting suspicious. Later she would tell me that she simply felt overcome by a sense of peace.

I opened the Bible to the spot I had bookmarked. The engagement ring was tied to the bookmark cord, so I gently untied it with shaking hands as I pretended to search for the verse I wanted. With the ring finally untied, I grasped it tightly with two fingers, took a deep breath and began to read.

As I read Ecclesiastes 4:12: "And a threefold cord is not quickly broken," I held up the engagement ring, which was a handmade white gold ring with a band that consisted of a threefold cord. As Karen stared at the ring with the verse echoing in her ears, I asked, "Will you marry me?"

Time seemed to stand still, as the verse, the ring, and the question sunk in. Karen reached for the ring and whispered "Yes!" as tears began to roll down her cheeks. I hugged her tight and we began to talk about what a perfect day it had been.

We walked back a couple of miles along the deserted beach. I say we walked, but in truth I'm not sure our feet were really touching the sand. As I later wrote in our online log, Casperson's Beach Cache became a cache we would never forget.

Found It!

Sonya Fazio

KrazyTrollz

Who would have thought a GPS, a few ammo cans, some goofy trinkets, and a walk in the woods would change my life?

I had heard about this activity called geocaching from a friend... Geo-what?! Yes, you know... high tech scavenger hunting using a GPS. Where you go look for stuff hidden in the woods. AND sometimes you find goodies you can swap out.

I was looking for something different to do and always enjoyed the outdoors so why not try it?

I was invited to go orienteering, another thing I had never heard of, and then was told we'd do that scavenging thing in the woods afterwards and go look for "stuff".

The orienteering thing was fun, and confusing, but it was nice doing something I normally wouldn't do. But then after that was over, I was handed this yellow gadget, told to look at the screen and 'FIND IT'. HUH?

It took some getting used to but I was able to follow directions and started heading in the direction the 'thing' told me to. And, when we got 'close enough' I was told to 'start looking'. To this day I don't remember what kind of container it was but it was big enough to drag some sticks off, open it, and find trinkets. I was so excited to have found this thing in the woods, sign a piece of paper, and look at stuff people left behind I wanted to do it again. And again we did. After we found a few, it started getting dark and it was time to go, but one thing was for certain: I was intrigued with a capital "I".

A few weeks later, the same friend asked me if I wanted to go to a geocaching campout weekend. I reluctantly agreed to go hang out with a bunch of strangers that hunted for these things in the woods and carried GPS units around with them. So, off to Parvin State Park in New Jersey we went. I met some incredibly nice people and did the same "Looking For Treasures" as before.

That Saturday evening, while folks were sitting around the campground chatting, I was sitting by the camper reflecting on the events of the day, when some tall blond guy came up to me, and said : "contrary to popular belief, women cheat more than men" while wearing a shirt that said "It's 10 PM, Do you know where your spouse is"? I wasn't sure if I was offended or amused and asked him why men liked women that treated them badly! We started talking about how long we each were Geocaching and about the group. . The whole experience was kind of annoying but we just kept talking. Until 2 am.

He still annoyed me the next morning, but came and found me. Then he handed me this "travel bug" thing and told me to take it close to where I lived. I took it and thought, He didn't even ASK me! Why am I doing this?!

But I wanted to find out what I was supposed to do with this "thing". So I took it. You'd think that the story would end there: with me holding the travel bug... But somewhere along the line at the camping event, I had given "that guy" my cellphone number... and the texts started.

My sister remembers me talking about this "Jim guy" all the time. My memories are different: I remember him being annoying.

The "Jim guy" and I got together a few months afterward to go caching with one of his friends. The next time we met up was without said friend. We started hanging out and going to events together. They say animals are a good judge of character; my parrots (feathered kids) liked him, so I figured he was probably okay. Eventually he moved to Pennsylvania

In November 2012, we were married. From caching partner to partner in life I would never have guessed that I would have met my husband in the woods when I wasn't looking for love, not even a little bit!

Thanks to this crazy scavenger hunt, we both "FOUND IT" - each other. This November we will have been married 3 years and in August will have known each other 10 years. It's a priceless gift.

Operation Treasure Hunt

Sonny Portacio

Team PodCache

Our story begins with a blind date. My friend Steve wanted to introduce me to his sister, Sandy and asked me if I wanted to come over to dinner. I replied "Uh, no, not really."

If things "didn't work out" I envisioned an awkward and uncomfortable situation. Instead, I offered a more casual and relaxed alternative. "It's called GEOCACHING," I told him and proceeded to describe this new activity that had captured my attention. He said it sounded like a good idea. So, a few days later, we all went geocaching. Sandy, her brother, his wife, and their three kids all came along on the "blind date" between Sandy and myself.

After many more geocaching expeditions, I realized I wanted to spend the rest of my life with her. I needed to come up with a unique way to propose. I needed something creative, meaningful and memorable. Geocaching seemed to be an eloquent, poetic, and meaningful way, and so the planning began...

I created a fake cache page by pasting together parts of a page and photocopying it. It looked slightly different from real cache pages, so I photocopied those as well for consistency. (Yes, it was before paperless caching!)

I created the cache container, painted it camouflage green, took it out in the back yard, sprayed it with a hose and tossed dirt on it to "age" it and make it look authentic.

I scouted out a location in San Diego and checked angles from which a photographer could capture the moment. I checked for entrance points and locations a lookout could be positioned. I timed the route we would need to drive. I took dozens of photographs of the location. I then recruited my accomplices: a lookout and a photographer.

Linda was the lookout for "Operation Treasure Hunt" and Gary was the guard/photographer. They hid the cache container, with the engagement ring inside, and Gary stayed to watch the cache. After all, I couldn't risk the ring – or the surprise!

Linda positioned herself down the road, with binoculars to spot our incoming car, and walkie talkies to notify Gary of our arrival. Once my car was spotted, he moved from guarding the container to the photo shooting position.

On the day of the proposal, I woke up early and a bit nervous, worrying about my sweating hands. But once I met up with Sandy for the day, all stage fright left me and I was absolutely fine! Now to execute the plan: Come up with things to do for the first part of the day, and then by any means, be at ground zero at 2:00!

We left for the day with too much time to burn. I needed to figure out strategies to stall and use up time. I was constantly sneaking looks at my watch.

While I drove, Sandy entered the coordinates to several caches into the GPS from the sheets that I handed her. We killed time browsing at REI but it was still too early. I took her to a photo spot and we snapped a few photos overlooking the San Diego bay. I've never experienced a day passing so slowly!

Finally it was time to head to the cache site. I drove slowly near "Linda's lookout" location to make sure my car was spotted. We got to the parking lot near ground zero and I saw Gary with a hat and sunglasses. I smiled as I knew that everything was going to be okay. We proceeded down to the cache area and Sandy followed the coordinates to the cache bush. I "spotted" it quickly and gave her the container to open and "log" the find.

Inside she found hundreds of small plastic colored rings and an index card that said, "choose one". She didn't immediately "get it", though she commented on the lack of a logbook.

Sandy picked out a purple plastic ring and I asked if that was REALLY the one she wanted and then she said, "Is there a REAL RING in here??" and started digging through the rings!

Finally she found the diamond solitaire, and I got down on my knee, told her that I loved her and asked her to marry me. I also repeated some words from the first card and flowers I had sent her: "I'm so glad I met you. Some events are life changing. Be Mine."

Of course she said YES and we kissed.

Then I began to tell her about the plan. I enjoyed watching her reactions as she heard the story unfold. My accomplices came down the hill and we all took a few more photos.

Sandy told me that to her the whole day seemed unplanned, like we were making it up as we went along. She had no idea about the precise time schedule I was following, and since I acted casual and nonchalant the whole day, she had no suspicions. Whew! The day was absolutely beautiful, clear, sunny, and warm at a perfect spot on the cliffs overlooking the beach.

Sandy and I were married later that fall and the following summer, I heard about something called podcasting. Since I'm a geek I wanted to create one. Sandy suggested we do it about something we knew and loved: Geocaching. PodCacher was born!

To find out more about PodCacher, hear more geocaching stories, and to connect with myself and Sandy head on over to www.podcacher.com

Caching on One Leg

Becca Hernandez

Monkey Trouble

In 2011, I became very sick and doctors could not seem to figure out what was wrong. Without going into too much gruesome detail, my illness (finally diagnosed as Antiphospholipid Antibody Syndrome) caused my right leg to be amputated below the knee. It also later caused three of the fingers on my right hand to be removed as well. (I've been through 48 surgeries since July 2011.)

After that, I was convinced that my geocaching life was over. How was I going to get to the caches I love to seek? How was I going to sign logs after having half of my dominant hand amputated?

I've been geocaching since 2008. I discovered the game through friends and immediately became enthralled – and addicted. It took me so many places like beautiful state parks, rich forests, historical monuments, and I saw a waterfall for the first time – all because of geocaching!

Then, in 2013 I met Toni, the person who changed my entire attitude – not only toward geocaching, but life in general. It was May; my mother had just passed away, I was looking for a place to live back in my hometown, and I was in a dark depression that I wasn't sure I was going to pull out of – constantly crying, pulling away from friends and family, and many dark thoughts I do not wish to discuss.

Toni made me see the sun again, she put a smile back on my face and in my heart. I was positive that no one would ever love me again, not in the state my body was in: right leg and three fingers gone, amputated. She gently and so easily showed me that I was wrong. Someone could love me – her!

The first subtle warning of Toni's feelings came when she threatened in front of a group of friends to push me, in my wheelchair, all the way from our home town to Lakeland, Florida to Geowoodstock 2013 (GC3K3YB) if I didn't agree to go. I had previously said that I wasn't going. I was convinced that this woman did not like me, yet here she was publicly declaring that she cared enough about me to make sure that I went and that I had a good trip regardless of the condition I was in.

This woman, this amazing and beautiful woman, who could have anyone she wanted spent the Geowoodstock weekend pushing me around in a wheelchair, through grass and dirt. After that, she was beside me for numerous surgeries, she was there when I received my new leg and walked again for the first time. The day we walked out of the doctor's office with my new leg, we got into the car, and she asked me "When do you want to go caching?"

Toni believed in me; she believed that I could and would do what I loved again. It took her a long time to make me believe as well. When we visited Homosassa Springs Wildlife State Park in Homosassa, Florida, she made me feel comfortable and strong enough to get on a boat. In the past, I was terrified of anything that floated on water. However, I trusted her enough and she believed in me enough that I could do it; and I did.

Later, at FDR State Park in Georgia, we attended Going Caching 2013 (GC407GG). I was still very new on my prosthetic leg, and could not do much walking. I was forced to sit in the car while everyone on our team went through the woods and did amazing caches to earn the A.C.E (Adventurer's Challenge Expedition) geocoin. At the end of the day, Toni could tell that I was upset that I could not actively participate. She promised me that I could and would the next year. And she was right!

At Going Caching 2014 (GC4AHKM), we completed, together, the Five Senses Challenge and both earned a limited edition geocoin. When we were faced with climbing the tower in Rome, Georgia, at Going Caching 2014, I was prepared to let her go it alone and wait for her at the bottom. She was not to be denied. She talked to me; she made me believe that I could do this, that I could climb three stories of stairs to see the beautiful view from the top. It took a very long time, a lot of rest, and mounds of determination, but I made it. We made it to the top together.

Toni helped me see that my life was not over after amputation. Geocaching helped me see the same thing.

The only day better than being able to walk to a cache again, was the day Toni and I were married in Washington, D.C. We even made sure to grab a cache on our wedding day! Toni and I are very active with events and our absolute favorite is "Going Caching" held in October in Georgia each year.

The doctor's saved my life by taking my leg. The prosthestist gave me a new leg. Toni gave me love and life again, but geocaching made me feel life again.

I get a lot of comments from fellow cachers. They call me an inspiration and motivating. I simply see myself as someone who did not want to give up this wonderful pastime. With the help of my amazing wife, of course!

Making the Kansas Heartland Geocaches

Ernie Cantu

cantuland

GeoArt wasn't an entirely new concept back in December of 2008, but it was pretty new. All I knew about GeoArt back then was from looking at a map of geocache icons for the ET Highway; that was good enough to start an idea forming for me.

I had a problem though: living in a Public Land Survey System state, there were roads running north-and-south and east-and-west everywhere around me, dotting the entire state with interfering one-mile squares. I didn't have room near me for drawing a simple shape with curves, such as over a nice big open desert or a state park with ample acres of wooded lands for hikers. How was I going to create the GeoArt I had in mind?

Could I fit it in one square mile of land? No, I encountered too much private land. Could I fit it in a few sections of land? No, "just a few sections" would not do; I needed more space. I spent lots of my time driving country roads and evaluating potential hiding spots, all the while trying to keep the grand plan a secret. My layout eventually encompassed an area six miles wide (east and west) and six miles tall (north and south) so that the outline of the shape crossed enough roads to plot out all of my dots at good hiding spots.

(Because what is the point of GeoArt if it's isn't also filled with good hiding spots? A simple power trail of micros would not do at all.)

Planning my GeoArt involved lots of hiding, moving, re-hiding, revising, and head scratching. I made plans to have the series published as a Valentine's Day gift… then a Mother's Day gift… even a Father's Day gift, maybe for her birthday, or for my birthday – but the changes seemed to go on and on. Would there ever be an end to all of this?

After almost two years of revisions, secret-keeping, and several short drives, the entire series finally reached successful completion and publication on October 2, 2010. It's a totally random day but my surprise was finally complete!

It was GeoArt worthy of my dream: showing the world the love for my wife.

It's a heart-shape GeoArt (which is just one aspect of the whole series.) Twenty-six geocaches make up the outline of the heart, one for each letter of the alphabet. At the time of publishing, every geocache led seekers to a black ammo box with a custom cantuland-geocache-logo painted on the sides. Each geocache was packed with excellent swag and had a unique car air freshener inside to prevent that all-too-common "ammo box smell." The series encompassed a mixture of traditionals, two-stage multi-caches and a variety of easy puzzles with a huge-size ammo box for a grand finale.

Each geocache in the series tells a separate story about our history together. Cache pages reveal to the world stories of our first date, our wedding, kids growing up, and adventures together on vacations. Each page has a link at the bottom to the next page in the series of stories. A good start on the pages is at http://coord.info/GCQAQQ for a cache called Heartland Geocaches.

When my GeoArt masterpiece of love was published, it was a total surprise – and she loves it.

A Surprising Tradition(al) Cache

Bekka Golenor

Bucket St James

In March 2015, I planned a short three day surprise birthday trip for my boyfriend, "Geo-LMP." He knew we were flying somewhere, but didn't know where until the week prior to our trip. I thought my surprise was a good one; turns out, his was much better.

We landed in San Francisco and the next day started like any typical vacation day, asking ourselves what caches are we going to find?

"Geo-LMP" said his caching friend, "jellis," had left him a geocoin to pick up and we needed to find it quick before someone else took it. After a delicious breakfast at our hotel, we caught the historic F-Train to Pier 39 around 10:00 am. Approaching ground zero we noticed a muggle sitting directly across from the cache site. Geo-LMP was a bit worried that the muggle was watching, but I was confident in our geocaching skills. . After some discussion, we decided to go for the cache.

"You grab it real quick, I'm going to put on my fleece," he said. It was foggy and a little chilly so I thought nothing of it as he started rummaging through his backpack while I grabbed the cache. Inside was a large envelope that said, "Do Not Open Unless You Are 'Bucket St James.'"

I looked at him questioningly, "I thought you said they were leaving something for you?"

He was grinning from ear to ear and sort of half-shrugged. "Open it," he said. I started to open the envelope and my hands were shaking as I pulled out the card. Such a beautiful card and inside was printed out words of love from him. I started to cry as I read. The last words were, "...now please look at me because I have a very important question to ask you." I looked up and he was kneeling before me with the most gorgeous ring I've ever seen.

"Will you marry me?" he asked.

"Yes, yes, a million times yes!" I answered.

Little did I know that the "muggle" who was watching was actually there to record one of the most important moments of my life! After the proposal, the "muggle" came over and introduced himself as "postman14." He told us he had caught the whole thing on phone's camera. "Geo-LMP" had been posting in a local cachers' Facebook group asking for assistance with pulling off this surprise proposal. He had been posting back and forth within the group finalizing details even the night before! I had no idea! Even the cache owner, "WarNinjas," was in on the plot and graciously allowed us to muggle the cache. (Hopefully the first and last cache we ever muggle!)

Thank you to all who assisted "Geo-LMP" and made this moment a success! It was truly a remarkable accomplishment, given the fact that he had less than a week to pull it all together. I am so lucky to share this hobby with the man I love, the man who will be my husband.

Stories of Adventure

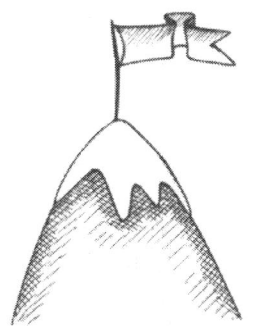

Geocaching in Prison

Christie Eckardt

LostintheClouds

After my first FTF on a new continent, I thought the day couldn't get any better. I was so wrong!

In search of another cache during our week-long winter vacation, my husband, two children and I set off under darkening skies toward a remote spit of the African island we are temporarily calling home. The road turns to gravel and soon the groundcover begins to reclaim even this small sign of civilization. A small path wide enough for a single car branches off to the left and my muggle husband says he'll wait there because there is no way to turn the car around once he enters.

My two kids and I set off on foot alone. Almost immediately the monsoon skies tear open and pelt us with rain. A blanket of interconnected spider webs supports hundreds of palm spiders, each nearly 4" in diameter, along either side of the trail. If not for the diamond-like raindrops in the webs, we'd walk headfirst into them.

We veer off onto a shadowy mud-choked path and even the birdsong falls silent. We start to whisper as we venture deeper and deeper into the thicket, taking care not to step on any branches or make any noise. We wonder how long it's been since anyone has used this path other than geocachers…

It seems like a good place to hide out if you are avoiding the authorities. What if we aren't the only people out here? The path turns left and suddenly we come upon a clearing which seems cheerfully bright in comparison to the dense forest. You can almost hear the fear evaporating as we enter the open area.

We laugh at ourselves as we turn left to follow the path. The jungle closes in tightly, forming a tunnel of dark green and we freeze as we come face-to-face with the ominous guard gates of the abandoned prison. It is as if the jungle itself is alive and swallowing something evil.

We instantly start freaking out, alone in the dark jungle in the rain. It looks like a horror movie set and my kids are ready to bolt but THAT MOMENT is when any hardcore cacher knows the real adventure begins.

My mom would *so* not approve.

What does it say about *my* maternal skills that I am making them stay? Something to think about... later.

he kids stay rooted to their spot in the clearing as I approach the building and cautiously peer into the guard towers' gaping windows. Strewn broken furniture and soaked papers lie scattered around a staircase. I creep upstairs to see if the cellblocks in the cache photos are up there. Nope.

Back down at the gate, my kids hesitantly approach as I slide the rusted lock open. Forcing the metal door inward lets loose an unholy screech across the jungle and all the birds take to the air. Great! Every serial killer within 10 miles now knows exactly where we are!

We step inside the gate and see a tiled courtyard which is rapidly being overtaken by the jungle – trees growing up through the cracks and roots stretching down from above. The cache is supposed to be right in front of us, but where are the cellblocks?

We walk 15 feet to the edge of the tree line and like a sunken ship coming hazily into view; the cellblocks emerge from the darkness. The row of pitch-black doors, like open mouths, stretch on in either direction behind prison bars. CREEPY FACTOR OVERLOAD! Maybe I'm not so hardcore after all.

We run, and I mean run, back to the car to get dad! We tell him just enough to convince him to come back with us, not the scary parts, and move quickly to stay ahead of our lingering fear.

Back at the courtyard, we plunge through the mosquito-laden blanket of air and thorny bushes scratching our legs, circumvent tangled clusters of barbed wire and ascend the steps to enter the cellblock walkway. We are glad to be out of the rain and I can't help but think – we are in an abandoned prison in an unpopulated jungle on an African island in a monsoon! I LOVE THIS GAME!

My husband is being eaten alive by the mosquitoes so we have to hurry. It's in cell #10 which is near the end. We approach and see rusty metal bunk bed frames in each cell but it's so dark inside we can't see to the back. Using my cellphone light, we see there is nothing else in there. Where is the cache?

Then I spot it – in a tiny round window near the ceiling in the back wall above the bunk bed... behind a giant female palm spider. My family looks at me and says, "You're the geocacher!" and hands me a stick as they step back to let me in. They offer to hold the light for me from the safety of the walkway.

I mentally compare the number of tetanus shots I've had to my age as I climb up the bunk bed frame. It is wobbly and I wonder if it will collapse and impale me. I picture my headstone reading "Died in Prison."

I stick to the outside edges where the rust will take longer to eat through and get to the cache guardian – my headstone changes to "Eaten by Freak Spiders in Prison".

I ask for her forgiveness and gently remove her with the stick to grab the cache. I make my way back along the bedframe to get outside for better lighting to sign the log and take pictures of my 200th cache!

My family then declares mutiny due to the bloodthirsty mosquito horde and runs off leaving me in the prison alone to replace the cache in the dark. It's then that I wonder where the angry spider might be lying in wait for me.

I manage to replace the container without feeling any legs crawling over me and emerge from the jungle with the biggest smile on my face ever!

Who Says Smoking Kills?

Jennifer Thrailkill-Leonard

catsimmie

We were in Marina Del Ray, California, and just had lunch with my brother. My son wanted to play on the playground and needing a smoke, I walked down to the water's edge away from the playground while my husband watched him. There was a family a ways down and that was it for people on the beach.

I was looking at my phone to see where the nearest geocache was when I saw a little girl in a cute pink dress and leggings walking towards the beach. I asked her, "Where's your momma?"

She pointed behind her and said, "Momma."

So I assumed her mom was close behind.

I looked back down at my phone and heard a loud splash. I looked up to see she had jumped in and was sitting in the water. I quickly look around and saw NO ONE else. At this point a small wave pushed her onto her back and she was screaming.

I rushed in and grabbed her as more waves were coming over her head since she couldn't get up. Now these were NOT big waves. These were mostly wakes as we were near the marina, but it was enough to push her down in the sand making it hard to get her up at first. Finally I grabbed the straps on the jumper-dress and jerked her up out of the suction. Her leggings and diaper stayed in the water and she was so scared she pooped everywhere! I don't blame her; I almost did the same thing!

So I picked her up normally and cradled her, asking where her momma was. She was screaming and crying and fighting me yelling and pounding on my chest: "You not momma! You no momma!"

So I figured she HAD to have come to the playground. She was Indian and the others from the beach were not. I'm carrying her up toward the playgroud, kicking and screaming. Finally her mom heard her and met us right at the edge of the playground. The girl saw her mom and said, "I swim."

Her mom freaked out! She had been talking to someone and looked away for a moment. I told her that was all it took and explained what happened. She was so apologetic and thankful so much so she kept slipping into her native language. I think it was Hindi? Even with her thick accent I knew what she meant. She took her daughter back, gave me a hug, and went to dry her off and change the little girl's clothes.

And thanks to the geocaching app, to give you distance, the playground was about 782 feet from where I was standing at the water's edge. I know that because the nearest cache called Beached Flatfish (GC5N8E7) was 815 feet and was located about 30 feet from the edge of the playground.

We left the playground to head toward an event, 'SFV Geocachers Meet & Greet #63' (GC5Q1TM) with wet capris and my soaked socks and shoes filled with sand. A small price to pay, that's for sure! Next time people complain about my smoking, I'll be sure to remind them that my smoking saved a child's life!

Our First FTF or A Fool-hearty Twilight Quest

Jessie Maxwell

jtcoffee

(co-conspirators: SGilly and yooper RJV)

When I lived in Michigan, I most frequently cached with two of my close friends. When we were together, we signed the logs as our personal geocaching names but we referred to ourselves as 'The Usual Crew'. We had many adventures – from tree climbing to steep hill descending, to falling in rivers to dodging leaping squirrels to confusing border patrol – and we always came back with smiles and stories to tell. However, one August evening in 2011 we achieved our proudest moment: our first First-To-Find.

The three of us taught summer camp at the time, so by late in the season, quiet evenings on the couch were relished. On the evening of August 30th, I was relaxing, jammie-clad, with my cat on my lap and my laptop close at hand. Just then my email notification pinged – a new cache had been placed. The Usual Crew had yet to achieve an FTF, so my ears perked up and my eyes opened wide. The fire of an eminent quest began to burn… disregarding the hour or so left of daylight, I sent messages to The Usual Crew, attempting to prod them back out into what I was sure would be guaranteed victory.

To be honest, I didn't leave much room for declining – that cache was ours… I could feel it! So I may have told them something like "You have to come!" Reluctantly – and first ensuring the other was coming as well – my two friends humored me and we made a plan.

The cache (GC336EV) is a multi, so two of us decided to meet near the first stage to do the math involved while we waited for our third counterpart to drive an hour back to the park where the cache was; thanks to the title of the cache, we at least knew it was in the local arboretum. Did we check the puzzle ahead of time? Did we figure out exactly where the first stage was? Of course not! Speed was our top priority with the waning light – the Arb was only open until sunset – so we practically ran from the car to the first stage. All the while we were picturing dozens of people (if not twice that many!) clambering for the cache so were borderline ecstatic to arrive to find no one around.

You know the burning urgency to be first, reminiscent of a youthful sibling rivalry? This fervor coursed through our veins as we attempted to calculate the last stage's coordinates. Haste kept causing us to have to retrace our steps and recalculate; the description sent us to a location with many possible numbers, and careful analysis of the description would probably have led any normally information-processing person to the proper set of numbers on the first try – with our exuberance equal to three espressos each we jumped to many conclusions which led us mathematically astray. The first stage calculations took us an excruciatingly long amount of time – we ended up finishing just as the third spoke of our Usual Crew wheel arrived.

We were sitting on a bench alongside a wooded trail to complete the coordinates when we heard someone shuffling at great speed down the hill toward us. Our friend had arrived, and much to our joy he was running – as fast as a man who frequently declared how he doesn't like to run – could. We thought he too had caught on to the thrill of the hunt, but as he approached he was bursting with news: apparently, as he was making his way down the trail to where we were, he had nearly collided with a hunting barred owl!

Seemingly both man and owl were fixed toward their goal, neither realized the other was there until they almost occupied the same space, and both were equally shocked at one another's presence. Being bird enthusiasts (to say the least), my friend and I were equally amazed and envious of this incredible wildlife encounter but had to quickly switch gears… now that we were all there and the final location's coordinates were in hand, we had to make a break for it since the daylight was fading.

We charged down the hill, listing out loud the various caching-nemeses we suspected were down there already taking away our victory. We threw all stealth to the wind as we flew down the trail past the twilight dog walkers and joggers. Our GPS lead us into a thicket with a little trail with lots of potential hiding places. At this point we felt the surge of energy that all geocachers feel when they've nearly made an exciting find.

But we kept coming up empty! The obvious places had been checked by each of us, two of us had thoroughly examined all crevices of a log, and we hit that point where you feel like you've searched everywhere twice. The realization that we might not make the find that night started to sink in, and we started discussions of meeting again the next morning at the crack of dawn, before work, to see if we could make the find. Just I had gone back to check the log again, one of us finally put their hands on a container we'd never seen before. Much to our joy, the log was blank – the first blank log we'd ever seen! – and if anyone was still left in the Arboretum as darkness was settling in, I am sure they heard our celebratory shouts as we jubilantly signed the log.

If there was ever any doubt that we would be geocachers for life, this evening's foray sealed the deal!

Another Name For Fun

Ivan Bissell

223irb

I can go geocaching near or far,
I can go on foot or in my car.

I've seen some sights only geocachers see,
Just follow the coords; that is the key.

As for myself, (and this might be braggin'),
I have hidden a geocache guarded by a dragon!

Under a rock or next to a tree,
It's hard to say just where it will be.

You must hunt for it and that's half the fun,
But you'll be rewarded when you are done.

Log all your caches, finds or not,
Summer or winter, cold or hot.

It's a year-round sport, growing in size,
An enjoyable way to get some exercise.

But don't take it from me, or any elf,
Get out there and do it for the good of yourself.

It's free to sign up so please don't ignore,
When that little voice asks, "What're you waiting for"?

Lake Mary's Curse

Kimberly Eldredge

TippySheep

It's a cloudy day. Dad is tense as we loading the truck. He's often tense when we're heading on a trip, even a day trip just across the state. I know he's going through his "mental list" – and this one is different. This list has things like 'tripod' and 'extra batteries'.

My list is simpler, a flowered swimsuit, the GPS, goggles, and cache page. Mom is in charge of practical things like towels and a change of clothes.

I'm thinking about mascara. I never wear the stuff since it makes my eyes itch and become red. But I'm wondering if I shouldn't put on makeup, lipstick, waterproof mascara. I attempt to tame my hair but it's breezy so I'm sure it won't matter.

I bounce in my seat the whole drive, chattering away, excited. I read the cache description (GC1VKZA) at least a dozen times:

"Took the kids to the lake today. As I sat pondering the beauty of Lake Mary I realized there isn't enough geocaches IN THE LAKE Mary area. So, I went into MacDiver mode, built and placed one. Although I tried not to get wet, it was inevitable considering I had the entire next generation of GCers with me."

And the hint: *"Anchor Chain, down under two-three feet"*

I've got this! I had been a competitive swimmer for years, can hold my breath for nearly two minutes, and I have my goggles and dad's waterproof flashlight. I keep imagining the look on my face when I pop up holding the cache...

At the lake we navigate what seems like all of Flagstaff, Arizona, trying to get in some last-days-of-summer fishing, boating, water skiing, and picnicking. I'm disconcerted at the sheer volume of muggles. (A bright pink swimsuit and on-shore camera crew don't exactly lend to the discrete.)

I really didn't need to worry about that. Nobody looks at us twice. There is some initial struggle trying to get the camera level on the tripod; this is very different than shooting in my own, level, evenly lit studio. We already decided not to even TRY for sound…

Dad wants me to look at the camera, look at the GPS, and then point into the lake at the buoy. Except after five takes it becomes apparent this is beyond my acting skills. I couldn't point at the buoy without looking at it and if I turn, I move completely out of the frame. We finally give it up as a bad job and I hand over the GPS and get ready to swim out.

I'm walking into the water, painfully aware of the camera looking at me. I've done videos before but this… well I'd never done video with no makeup, an uncontrolled environment, and I'm in my bathing suit, for crying out loud! Even though the water is warmer than I expected, I still have my shoulders pulled up around my ears; I don't want to put my arms in the water. I remember I'm being filmed; this slow-walk into the water has to be beyond boring. I pull my goggles into place and swim.

There are weeds in the water. Long trailing weeds that look like hair. The blue-tint on my goggles, so nice in a white-bottomed swimming pool, makes everything darker. And I can only so easily imagine that the weeds actually are hair…

By the time I reach the buoy, only about 30 yards from shore, I'm shaking. The weeds are tangled around my arms and legs, feeling for all the world like hair. The long hairs of creatures long dead…

Unbidden, the images from the Harry Potter lake scene rise in my mind… The way the Inferi, the bewitched dead bodies, were hurling themselves at Harry and Dumbledore, out of the water, long hair flailing and whipping, skeletal hands reaching, the way they appeared from the gloom in the water…

I hang on the buoy, gasping for air even though it was a short swim and I had taken it slowly. I peer back toward my parents on shore. I can't see them without my glasses but it looks like mom has her arms crossed, tense. I already know dad didn't like my plan – but then, neither of them swims.

I'm surprised by the size of the buoy; it's much bigger than it looked from shore. And it goes down a good two feet in the water. I switch on the waterproof flashlight and shine it at the anchor chain.

The beam hardly pieces the gloom. Between the overcast day, the blue on my goggles, and all the slit stirred up from the boaters, the water is little more than murk. The chain is clearly dirty; the slightest touch leaves streaks of rust on my skin like blood.

Aware the camera is still rolling, I take a breath and dive. I quickly realized the flashlight beam is only good to about 6 inches. I can't look from here and see anything. I surface. Another deep breath, down again.

Even though I can swim underwater and have great breath control, my heart is racing and my ears are telling me I'm deep-deep. I know it isn't the truth.

I can hear my folks asking me from shore if I'd found it. I yell back no and fell down the chain with my feet. Another dive. Another. Another. I'm frustrated and trying not to let my fear get to me. It's just water. Depthless. Dark. Filled with dead bodies and hair and blood– I stop that train of thought.

One more dive. This time I hold the flashlight in one hand as I pull myself down the chain. Down. The water is getting darker and colder. The pressure in my head says 4 feet, then 5. It's dark. I can hear the blood in my head but the boat motors are muffled. 6 feet. 7. 8. I'm at the end of what I can really dive comfortably. One more foot, still looking…

And then…

Ahhhhhhhh! I'm racing toward the surface, the water getting lighter and warmer, my lungs burning. I'm cursing the stupid water shoes that are keeping me from the strong kicks I want.

At the surface, I'm gasping for air. As I swim back to shore, my dad asks if I find it. I stop, tread water, and pull my goggles off my face. And drop the waterproof flashlight. *Dad's* waterproof flashlight. I can see in his face that he can see in mine that it's gone. He suggests for a moment that I look for it – in 12 feet of murky water with rocks and dead-hair weeds and it's *off* so it's not like it is glowing.

I don't even try.

I swim back to the truck. Towel off. Dad packs up the camera, mom is worried because I can't seem to get warm. We go to a nearby campground so I can shower – the blood-like rust marks don't come off.

This is geocaching; sometimes you don't find the cache. Sometimes the pike get the flashlight. But dad bought me lunch and eventually the rust washes off.

And you put it on YouTube anyway.

An Adventure In Retail

Dale Swinehart

Dale n Barb

Barb and I learned about geocaching in March of 2006. We went out the very next day after and found our first cache only two tenths of a mile from our house, hidden in a wildlife sanctuary. Since that fateful first day, we have found and hidden many caches and met many great friends during that time.

But we are most proud of our contribution to geocaching on the Space Coast of Florida.

Barb and I used to own and operate an automotive air conditioning parts store in which we had some extra room that was not being used. In 2007, Barb suggested that we use that small space to carry a few geocaching supplies. We contacted Groundspeak and became an authorized distributor and were soon stocking some supplies for local cachers. We called this the Space Coast Geocaching Store. We also formed the Space Coast Geocachers Association.

It was a really big change from running an automotive A/C business to running straight retail! I know that Barb and I both had our share of sleepless nights! Retail can be tough – no matter what. But to be running a store that catered to geocachers… It was a leap of faith!

Some of our friends even worried that we'd gone off the deep end. How much money could be made from such a narrow-niche store?

But when a geocacher would walk in – some from another state or even another country – and start browsing the original walk in geocaching store in all of the United States, we knew it was all worth it!

Guess what?

We have since closed the A/C business and now only operate the Space Coast Geocaching Store!. We even had lackeys from Groundspeak visit and do a video of our store.

Our love for geocaching and the geocaching community shows with our dedication to owning and operating a "brick and mortar" store for cachers from all over the world to visit. I know it might not seem like an "adventure"

– there are no angry bears, rattle snakes, or near-misses with Officer McFriendly – but it's been the biggest and most rewarding adventure of our life. Barb and I love helping geocachers from Florida, and all over the world, "Take Pride In Your Hide!"

Turning of the Tides

Maude Stephany
Family Extremes

Neap Tide

Twice we've come, and twice we've gone, and twice returned empty handed.

Twice prepared, and twice not scared, and twice we were almost branded -

by the river, that fateful river, that rises and falls with the tide -

by the river, that brown sludge river, by which we live beside.

Ebb Tide

The Fraser River heard the words, "Family Extremes is on the move,

twice we have come, and twice thou hast won, and now we come our mettle to prove.

If thou leave not this tiny channel in the time of the moon's wanin', then soon thou shalt be set upon by one plus three, who seek a curious tree."

Though night was dark, the meadowlark did call, mayhap it was thunder

The river cried, "No! I fear I must go under –

for fearsome four approach-eth now. I dare not come a-ground."

And so, when we did set out, the route was dry we found.

"The night is full upon us, though fire lights the dark

let us go forth and prove our worth and try to find the mark."

Our foursome crept where once the depth of river had advanced

we came prepared for we had dared and would not take a chance.

When fire flamed, we were not scared, instead we danced in glee.

"I see the flame of which was spoken," said our little she.

So search-ed we, where treasure be, and soon held it in hand

We won the treasure, we took its measure, and then surrendered it to land.

As 'ere we left, the bats did dance a merry jubilee.
As four set forth, four took leave, and somewhere... is that tree.

Midspring's Night Dream

Kent Van Cleave

psyprof

I met my girlfriend, Cyn, at a geocaching event. How was I to know it was the start of an epic romance – and epic geocaching adventure! Soon we were out geocaching together at every opportunity.

Cynwood and I were working on the East Tennessee Elders Challenge (GC2JKMP), for which we must find the oldest cache in a number of east Tennessee counties. We were at Coker Creek Village for a memorial service for a friend, Scott Crisp, and decided to go get this cache afterwards. Since we were so close to Polk county, a county neither of us had discovered a geocache in, we decided to go a little further and find a Polk County cache. And what better cache to go after than one that has withstood the test of time, the Elder Cache of the county?

Arriving in the area after 5 p.m., we found the gate to access the boat ramp near where the cache is hidden closed. So we drove to the overlook on the bluff above the area and took the trail down, then the road. We got the Boyd Creek Trailhead cache on the way down, and did the Whitewater River Earthcache first stage.

As we proceeded down the trail at the start, we began to hear distant thunder. I knew there were thunderstorms in the area, and expected some could be pretty rough. We decided to press on, since I was certain the storms would mostly miss us to the north. Still, the threatening thunder gave us cause for concern on our way down. We threw the camera into cynwood's backpack and prepared for the worst, including checking out the toilets in the picnic area just in case we needed a place to shelter.

Zeus decided to have mercy on us though and left us alone.

On the way down, we enjoyed a profusion of spring flowers. As we were walking, we discussed the possibility of returning in a couple of months to pick huckleberries, as they were in profusion all around us, blooming madly.

The first thing we did at the river was take the measurements for the Whitewater River History earth cache. Then we set off down the trail towards the Boyd's Gap cache (GC3C99). We arrived in the vicinity just at dark. As we searched, a whippoorwill began calling, 40 or 50 feet from us. I have always loved whippoorwills, and used to creep up on them at dusk so I could watch them. So this added to the adventure for me. I was able to call it to within ten feet, but then it flew off up the river. He was close enough we could hear him moving around in the brush.

We searched for the cache for about 30 minutes, to no avail. Then we decided to test our assumption as to which side of the trail to search, by flashlight, and in less than five minutes I was opening the cache. One more Elder Cache down, but still a way to go to get back to the car, and all of it uphill.

Moments of transcendence are all around us, if we will only recognize them for what they are. They lie more in the experience of simple moments than on some grand stage, come up softly before us, rather than with a fanfare. In order to experience them, we need only be fully in the present, then recognize them for what they are.

We started back for the overlook in deep darkness. The thunderstorms had bypassed us, except for a brief sprinkling, but cloud cover remained. As we set off back towards the car, we passed through several places where masses of lightning bugs were flying around. These are not of the blinking sort, but the sort who turn on their lights for five to ten seconds at a time. I had never seen so many lightning bugs before! They were showing off their marvelous skill everywhere we looked. Imagine standing in a still, dark, dense forest, with no moon and no stars, surrounded by dozens of green lights slowly streaking across your field of vision.

This was truly one of those transcendent moments.

We turned off the flashlights, enchanted, and stood for long moments, watching this unfold.

Then, not too far away, a great horned owl began to call. It was a lonely echoing call, at once foreboding and comfortable. We stood quietly in a dense, dark forest, surrounded by an amazing light show, and enjoyed the owl's concert.

Eventually, we made our way back to the overlook and the car. Cyn noted that the clouds had cleared, and there was an amazing celestial display at our disposal. We stood there in the dark, arms around each other, gazing at the stars, for some long moments. Cyn commented that she wished she could see a satellite, as she has not seen one in nearly 20 years.

Within five minutes, I spotted a satellite, apparently in a polar orbit, streaking across the sky, bisecting Ursa Major. Manifest it and it will happen! Cyn set up her tripod and camera, with her largest telephoto lens, and photographed a planet, possibly Mars, as it looked red.

We thank the cache owner for putting this cache in such a beautiful area. It truly was a magical evening and well worth every minute that we spent here. TFTC!

Black Hills Adventure

LA Newell

J&LA

The first time I heard about 'Buzzard Drop Cache' (GC57F9) in the Black Hills of South Dakota, I wanted to go. It was about 420 miles away as the crow flies, and my hubby, "J", was not at all interested in the heights involved. I'd previewed the cache page countless times for a solid year before determining it was time to get it whenever the next group headed out. Since I'd never traveled or cached solo before, I posted a note on Facebook and found a fellow female cacher only two hours away, BransonAdventure, whom I'd met only briefly once, was interested in going along with her teen daughter.

It was a frightening proposition to share my vehicle with a stranger, but she was cool. We met in a town along the way, hopped into my new-to-me, 4-wheel SUV as a "team", and off we went. Turns out Mrs. Branson was practically my long-lost sister. She was exactly the person who I needed to take on this trip. We'd both been through the same crazy experiences in life and share the same quirky personality; we became instant friends to this day.

Reaching Rapid City that evening, we got turned around while caching in Blackhawk through the Black Hills National Forest just as the sun was setting. Since we had no flashlights with us, we relied solely on the light of the GPS to guide us back. It certainly didn't help that my phone with its precious satellite maps had died when my service dropped over 300 miles back, nor that the last cache we attempted in the blackness was entitled Hornet Nest (GC3CJJV).

Ever try navigating unfamiliar territory over Ponderosa pine needle-covered rocks on a steep incline in the pitch dark with a bad ankle in thinner-than-usual air? Oh yeah, that was definitely interesting. We relied on one another and Branson's local family member to get through. We walked away with just that one DNF. At least there were no stings from blindly reaching under the rock ledge.

We returned to civilization where I discovered what looked like a wolf in the background of one of the photos I took of my new friend at one of the more difficult cache sites. For a second there I held my breath looking at it, but determined it was probably just a freaky-looking rock. It seriously was that dark out, so there could very well have been one standing there watching us we hadn't seen. I shudder to think.

We stayed the night at the relative's mountain-view home, eating pizza and telling stories before settling in, and then we set out the next morning for the vivid sapphire waters of Pactola Reservoir to meet Eskoclimber and the rest of the crew. We switched drivers up in the mountains to let the more experienced, newly named mtngoatmorava drive us through the rough backroads and the gates of the Wharf Gold Mine. Trusting my truck to someone I'd just met was a new one for me. Along the wild, muddy MMR, there were a couple sections that'd overflowed onto the road from nearby waterholes, so I'm glad we didn't end up in a pond! (That mud remained on my truck for months because I didn't have the heart to wash it off.)

Upon arrival, I was the first to hop out and stand at the precipice. The yawn of the canyon before me was more expansive in 3D and two tiers deeper than anticipated. I got a bit overwhelmed that I was finally seeing it in person. Although it was very windy at the cliff side, Eskoclimber was awesome and put everyone at ease as he talked us through every step, then dropped us each gently off the cliff. He was nice, patient, and such a professional; it was profoundly easy to trust our lives to him. It helped knowing his gear was good. In the most friendly yet stern way he warned, "Step on my ropes, and I'll step on your GPS." All this coming from a skinny man in a funny cowboy hat with a "lucky doll" strapped diagonally across his chest. Loved that guy!

One problem did crop up early on. Mtngoatmorava got a big gash on the back of his hand from bashing into the sharp rocks on his way down, but between my first aid kit and the skill of our guide, the day was able to continue. His injury was somewhat serious and bled through his dressings twice, but despite this he still became the belay for the rest of the group when he probably should've gone for stitches. Thanks to his help and the overwhelming dedication of everyone involved, most cachers including all three of us girls got to rappel twice, which was wondrous and scary! The second time I was brave enough to lean out from the very top of the ledge and was confident enough to wave at the camera halfway down. We took scenic photos of each person navigating the side of the jagged cliff, marveled at the spectacular view of Spearfish Canyon, and watched momof6furballs overcome an overwhelming fear of heights. I even got some valuable one-on-one lessons "learning the ropes," which I now use to set safety lines for myself on tricky terrain.

If this wasn't amazing enough, after saying goodbye to all but one member of the rappelling group, a cacher named SDHI, we followed his ATV along the backroads to tackle a nearby cache at the peak of Ragged Top Mountain. After finding safe routes through the narrow breaks in the rock face, we hiked up the steep terrain, encouraging one another along the way. At different points, we each had moments of weakness where we wanted to quit, but we talked each other through all the way up to the beautiful, rocky top.

It all came down to trust. Allowing others to be my safety net and becoming one for other cachers on this trip was such an exhilarating experience, just as grand as the actual act of rappelling off a cliff and navigating a mountain. We proudly stood at the summit near Ragged Top Romp (GCQPMD) and marveled at the gorgeous autumn colors below before hiking back down, thanking everyone we met, and driving all the way home that same night.

What an unforgettable trip!

Lewis Hills Geocaching Event

Ralph Schuessele

res2100

I enjoy hosting a number of geocaching events each year, ranging from the family fun picnic style events to the extreme such as events that involve over 50 kilometers of hiking over rugged terrain. Events are a great way to meet other like-minded individuals. And for the extreme events – like one on top of the highest mountain in Newfoundland, Canada – they ensure I am not hiking alone!

My wife, daughter, and I were vacationing in Newfoundland; after studying maps I came across Lewis Hills and the highest point, The Cabox. I had previously enjoyed hiking the 30+ kilometers round-trip to the highest point in Ontario: Ishpatina Ridge. The Cabox, at 814 meters above sea level, would be a 28 kilometer round-trip hike – and quite a different experience from Ishpatina Ridge.

At least I didn't have to worry about encountering any snakes, as I was told there are no snakes in Newfoundland... whew!

Despite some initial interest from others, it turned out that I would be making the hike alone and the only person at my geocaching event. I called it The Cabox (Lewis Hills) Picnic (GC2MBTE) and had planned to lead my fellow geocachers to the highest point in Newfoundland. From the summit of The Cabox we'd sign the event log, enjoy a picnic, and claim victory!

I made the hour-long drive to the trailhead, but now I was alone and in unfamiliar territory, always wondering, hoping I would bump into someone else along the way! Or that someone would be joining me at my event. I had published it as a geocaching event, after all!

The first kilometer was through a wooded area with a muddy trail. It was boggy and I already had wet feet. But after that, I was out in the open for the rest of the way.

The trail was marked in different ways: white rectangular markers on metal posts or swept gravel trails lined by rocks or just marked with rocks sitting on top of large boulders. I lost the trail too many times to count over the journey, but fortunately I had the trail on my GPS to at least keep me somewhat close to where I should be – even though I often wound up being 100 or more meters off.

This is a remote place and just wasn't travelled often. (And no, I didn't see any snakes!)

The main obstacle was the Fox Island River. It was around 10 meters wide and less than knee deep. I walked part way across the river bed stepping on rocks, but when I got to the main part, I made the decision to take off my shoes and socks, and wade across.

Ouch! Not a good choice! After making it part way across, my feet were hurting from the round rocks in the river. I fell forward into the river and got almost totally soaked. I scrambled to my feet and finished crossing. I left my partially wet shirt on and put on my raincoat over it – it was the only dry thing I had! At this point I no longer had any doubts about why I was doing this. This incident made me more determined to achieve my goal. Hiking cold and wet is hell, but I wasn't going to let it stop me!

My favorite part of the adventure was hiking along a mountain stream which flowed through the rising valley for several kilometers. The water in the stream was crystal clear and formed a number of small waterfalls and pools. The landscape was like nothing I had ever seen before. There were small waterfalls coming off the mountains along with patches of snow. I felt like I was walking through heaven. It was so beautiful here. I could have spent the whole day, but I still had a long hike ahead of me.

As I continued to ascend the mountain, I encountered a huge rock field. It consisted of light brown rock that looked like petrified wood, black lava rock which made me wonder if there was ever a volcano here millions of years ago, and boring greyish rock. These rocks were all mixed together and of various sizes. I wondered how these different types of rocks came to be all in one place. It was like God had shaken up a bunch of different rocks in a huge bucket and dumped it down the side of the mountain. I felt like I was walking through a barren wasteland from another planet.

Once I was out of the valley, I was rewarded with stunning views of the mountain range and far reaching views towards the Port au Port peninsula over 40 kilometers away. There were many small lakes and blankets of snow. Again I was in another new world! Every bit of the adventure brought a different experience and different sights.

The anticipation and excitement grew as my destination was finally in sight. 11:56 am, I MADE IT!

It took me 4 hrs and 26 minutes to hike approximately 12.5 kilometers. Somehow, by losing the trail so often, I saved 1.5 kilometers of hiking!

The views were breathtaking in all directions. I looked back from where I came and was in awe as to how far I had gone. It was a great feeling to be at the highest point in Newfoundland. Time to enjoy a nice picnic lunch as part of my solo geocaching event and reflect on everything I had been through just to get to this point.

I was looking forward to getting back to my wife and daughter. Originally I told them I probably wouldn't be back until 10pm or later, but the entire journey was a lot quicker than expected. Back across the snow and rock fields, down the slope of loose gravel, sliding and catching myself a couple times. Back along the stream through the valley – which I considered to be my special place of heaven. I crossed the river again but kept my shoes on (they were still wet from my first crossing!)

I made it back to where I parked, safe and sound, and with another amazing experience and event behind me. The entire adventure took just under 12 hours. My wife was surprised to see me back so early. The smile on her face when she saw me –and the hug I got – made me feel just as wonderful as when I made it to the top of the mountain.

Of the 16,000+ geocaches that I have found, this geocaching event ranks up there as my top 5 favorite of all time. The terrain on the Lewis Hills was unique, the panoramic views spectacular, the sights along the way amazing, the weather was perfect, and I got priceless memories that will last a lifetime.

Bobbing for Bob

Karen Allendoerfer

karenlona

I gasp and dive, face-first. My goggles aren't leaking, and I don't feel nearsighted. But the water is a muddy green, and I can barely see the rope. I grab the top and recoil from its slimy feel. My hands slip and dislodge bits of algae as I kick my feet through the surface of the water. I feel air on my toes.

I surface quickly to see a row of young men free-styling towards us. Suddenly I see G and myself from their point of view: a middle-aged couple in ill-fitting spandex, lurking next to this buoy, bobbing up and down.

G looks at me expectantly. "Nope," I say. "I can't even get down there." He nods and dives into the water.

He is down there a while, longer than I was. The swimmer dudes reach the level of the buoy and turn around, heading back towards shore. G comes up empty-handed. "It's a carabiner," he pants between breaths. "Uh… uh… uh-tatched to the concrete on the bottom, the same place the buoy is. I used the buoy rope to pull myself down."

"Ok," I say, more brightly than I feel. "I can try that." I fall forward, grab a fistful of algae-rope and pull, harder this time. My feet submerge but my body still pulls toward the surface. I'm fighting physics, feeling my cheeks and lungs full of air.

I'm supposed to be the stronger swimmer. I was on the swim team in high school. But I never liked to be under water. There was that time in lifesaving class when I was trapped under water with somebody else's arms around my neck, my own arms dog-paddling furiously. I could see the surface: the reflected light, people's arms and legs around it, waving through streams of blue bubbles, but I couldn't reach it. Instead of saving my friend Brenda like I was supposed to, I ended up breathing in water and choking. Afterwards, Brenda had apologized profusely. She hadn't known I was in trouble, she said. She was just trying to act like a real victim would have.

I am near the bottom of the rope. I can see the sandy bottom, the rope ending in the concrete. My hands fumble at the link. There's the carabiner. And then I hit the wall. There are 8 feet of water between me and breath.

Heart pounding, I head for the surface. It takes too long to get there. My husband's legs, his blue bathing shorts billowing out with water, his belly button, all flash by, and I burst out with a splash.

"I can't… do… it" I say. "I want to go back to the beach." G nods and wordlessly follows me back to shore. I swim my swim team stroke, the breaststroke, but without putting my head in the water. I hear the gym teacher in my head yelling that if this was real, Brenda and I would both be dead. I just keep swimming. My heart rate and breathing slowly return to normal, in time with my stroke. I finally remember that I'm in Hawai'i, on vacation, and that this is supposed to be fun. I sit on the beach and play with the sand for a while until G clambers up the beach and sits down heavily beside me.

"I know I said I'd try to help you find this cache," I say to G, "But I'm feeling like it's the Rubik's Cube cache all over again."

"What was wrong with the Rubik's Cube cache?" he asks. "You solved it, didn't you? We were FTF!"

"Yeah, I guess, but when we stopped for it I'd been sleeping in the car, and I was feeling crappy, and I kind of just wanted to get home. But you insisted we still had to stop and I had to do it. Why couldn't you just do it?"

"You did it so much faster than I would have! And you were the one who knew how to solve the Rubik's Cube."

"Yeah, with a solution book. And then after we logged it that guy complained about me using the book, and said he thought it was cheating … it just ruined the whole thing for me. Like other people don't get help when they need it." I sound whiny to my own ears. I stop talking and listen to the waves instead.

"Look," he says. "I think I can do it. I have enough air. I can't get down there on my own, but I can pull myself with the rope."

"I don't have enough air," I say.

"Come back out with me," he asks. "Let's try again."

I don't answer. I just sit there. One of the other swimmers — a guy in a baseball cap, separated from the pack and silhouetted against the sky — is walking by. "How're you doin'?" he asks, affably.

"Good," we both answer, almost in unison, and chipper.

The guy pauses and asks us about why we're in Hawai'i and what we're doing here on this beach. I let G explain geocaching to this particular muggle. I don't trust myself not to sound bitter.

"So, there's one out there attached to that buoy," G is saying. "It's called Bob."

"Bob?"

"Yes, the geocache is called Bob."

Involuntarily I conjure mental pictures of both my father, whose name is Bob, and my witty, urbane former coworker, also named Bob. One of these Bobs offers me a virtual martini, and I take it.

"And you're going to find it together?"

"Yes, that's the plan," says G. "We left the kids back at the house."

"How long have you been married?" asks the guy.

"Seventeen years," he answers.

"I'm getting married next year," he offers. "What's your secret?"

G and I look at each other.

"Doing things together like finding caches?" It seems like he expected this question to be easier for us to answer.

"I think you have to marry the right person," G says.

"Well, good luck," he says, touching the tip of his hat and wandering off down the beach toward his other buddies.

"You too!" we call after him.

When he has gone, we get up and swim back out to the buoy. We are the only ones left in the water. The sun is getting closer to the horizon. G dives again, and this time when he comes up he is holding a yellow tube. "I got it!" he calls. I take his hand, and we swim back to shore with Bob, together.

A Real Cliff Hanger

Val Sapirman

Radish61

You can't tell me geocaching isn't an exciting, thrilling game of worldwide exploration.

My daughter Chelsea and I found out how truly exciting the game could be while on a soccer trip in Scotland. While the rest of the family was off touring a castle in Edinburgh, Chelsea and I were focused on hunting down a multi-cache in that same city. Timing was going to be the most important factor for us since we had to be back to the tour bus to rejoin our family and group prior to their departure from Edinburgh.

We quickly programmed the coordinates for the first cache location into the GPS and set off on our adventure. Finding the first location was a breeze for the two of us, being that we were seasoned geocachers! What we were not so sure about was the manner in which we would retrieve the next set of coordinates in our multi-cache mission. This first location brought us to a small hole in the ground in some underbrush.

Neither Chelsea nor I had any desire to stick our hand into this hole in the ground to retrieve the cache container. What to do? Luckily, we had brought with us some tour brochures that we quickly rolled up to use as a retrieval tool. Wouldn't you know it – it worked! Out came a small film canister which contained the treasured next set of coordinates.

After programming the new location, we set off for part two of our adventure. The second location was more magnificent than we would have ever imagined. There we were in this beautiful park, in the center of the city, standing on the edge of a cliff overlooking lush foliage. The view was picture perfect.

The only issue… we needed to be a few feet off the cliff in mid-air to be at the actual cache coordinates. The cache couldn't be in mid-air, right? The clock was ticking and time was running short. We searched the area all around where we were and kept coming up empty. We both agreed that we would search for about 10 minutes more which would be the final limit prior to us departing for our return back to the bus.

Five minutes went by... still no luck. Seven minutes had passed... and the lightbulb finally went on. We checked the clue as a last resort. Well what it told us was that we were actually standing right on top of the cache box. It was right below our feet the entire time that we were admiring the view from the cliff's edge. Hidden under a section of dried grass and dirt was the prize we so desperately sought.

We quickly dropped off a travel bug for a Boy Scout troop from the US, signed the log sheet, grabbed a prize, sealed the box, re-stashed the cache, and made a run for the bus. We made it just in time and boy, what a story we had to tell. This was the first of our international geocaching adventures and many more are yet to come!

Concert on a Waterfall

Cyn Williamson

cynwood

The summer of 2014, my boyfriend and I went on a geocation adventure through the New England states, as well as into Ontario and Quebec, Canada. My boyfriend had already found caches in 40 of the 50 states and his goal was to complete the continental USA by the summer of 2014. Before leaving on our journey, we did some extensive research to plan a route best suited for an exciting geocaching adventure.

A goal for many hard core cachers is to complete the Jasmer Challenge, which requires finding a cache that was placed during every month since geocaching began. The Spot (GC39), which is one of the oldest caches in existence, was placed during the first month of geocaching, so it filled in the first month for both of us and was at the top of both our "must have" lists. If we did not get this cache, we would have to travel out west to meet the requirement, a journey of more than 1,000 miles each way

We set out to find the spot on my birthday, and since it was geocaching that first brought us together, we were very excited to share this adventure on this special day. Located in the Finger Lakes region of New York, The Spot took us a little off of our path, but was worth every minute.

Upon arrival at the parking coordinates, we noticed a man preparing to hike out on his own. He was carrying a large 22 pound pyramid and a didgeridoo. We were intrigued by his odd array of hiking gear, and felt certain that he had to be on some kind of spiritual journey. We introduced ourselves and made quick friends with Logan. Since he was familiar with the area he invited us to hike along with him. Before we left however, my boyfriend, psyprof, quickly grabbed his Jew's harp out of our car.

First we visited a waterfall, which was Logan's destination. We followed the water quite a ways, maneuvering along the rock wall, and crossing back and forth across the stream. Finally we reached the place Logan was looking for. Here, the stream changed from a gracefully flowing meander to a straight-drop waterfall of about 50 feet. Logan explained that according to legends, Indians believe spirits enter the earth at this very point. Logan said he wanted to bring his pyramid here, which he called an orgone collector, so that it could collect some of the positive energy. As we relaxed and enjoyed the beauty of this unique place Logan started playing his didgeridoo, and before long psyprof joined in with his harp. I was treated to an amazing, unplanned concert on the edge of the waterfall.

After Logan felt his pyramid had collected enough energy, we continued on our journey until we came to The Spot. Although the cache brought us here, the breathtaking view held our attention. Located near ground zero, was a large rock jutting out from the side of the mountain, overlooking a heavily forested valley. The two men sat on the rock, and Logan gave us a lesson on the construction of orgone pyramids. As a long-time maker of these unique pyramids he was more than happy to share his experiences with us. The pyramids contain metallic elements, such as gold and copper foils, and crystals, which collect and store the orgone energy. As a professional photographer, I welcomed the opportunity to take photos of yet another beautiful view!

Then it was time to search for the cache, which was still hiding nearby.

Psyprof and I walked in circles, trying to zero in on the coords... Then Logan shouted "I found it!"

As I was rummaging through the contents of the cache, a miniature pyramid Logan had secretly been carrying in his pocket was tossed in. At first I was stunned by his gesture, but he told me it was for us, and so I quickly grabbed it back out. As we signed the log, Logan entertained us with another tune on his didgeridoo.

This was a very special cache on a very special birthday, and not a second of this adventure will ever be forgotten. We were so glad to have met Logan. He helped turn a caching experience into something unique, and I can still hear the music playing when I look at the pictures I took that day.

On a Stormy Day

Keri Barnes
KBsta

On a stormy day, in the month of July,
We headed to Peyton, just the puppy and I.

Peyton's a prairie, away from the city
Nothing to look at; the landscape ain't pretty.

Geocaches a' plenty, the really big cool ones,
The little sized nanos aren't as much fun.

As I was driving, the wind was blowing around.
I decided to keep going, for no caches I'd found.

It was starting to sprinkle, soon then it was rain,
You don't get a "smiley" staying home in this game.

I noticed the hail now; it's getting real bad.
The sky's all dark and that cloud's looking mad.

I think we need shelter, the lightning is scary.
The branches are falling; this storm's getting hairy.

Next thing that happens, I still can't believe it…
The sound of a freight train, you cannot conceive it.

The pressure is pushing my car all around;
Thank heavens it stays there, never leaving the ground.

It felt like forever, there under that tree,
The lightning, the hailing, my puppy, and me.

No sooner it started, as I started to cry,
The whole stupid storm cloud returned to the sky.

As I rolled down my window, to see where to go…
The reward I was given, a vibrant rainbow.

As I drove back to the city, no caches I'd find,
Instead, I had a story, and a photo all mine!

Good Lock

Brian Klinger

KBLAST

"What?! You did the cache without me?!!"

Those were the first words out of my mouth when I found out that two of my best friends had been the first people to find the geocache, Good Lock (GC3426N). It was a cache placed by a user who, according to his profile, had never found a geocache.

There had recently been a rash of "sock puppet" accounts in our area, where well-known cachers would publish caches under an alternate username in order to remain anonymous. This anonymity often allowed the users to do or say cruel things without being caught, so this cache was met with skepticism by the geocaching community at large. There was even a rumor going around that I was the fake user, so that added to my interest in "Good Lock", and my concern.

"Well, we wanted to get First to Find, and even though no one was logging it, we knew there were lots of people checking the cache out."

Even though I was a little disappointed, I could understand. I asked, "So what was the cache like?"

After a bit of uncomfortable shuffling, they said, "Like nothing you've ever done before. We don't want to give anything away. It was AMAZING, but we're not sure we're recommending it, so that's all we're going to say."

My friends and I had done HUNDREDS of geocaches together, ranging from tree climbs, to field puzzles, to tunnel crawls, to the absurd. This statement added to the intrigue, but kept me concerned enough to wait until I could attempt the cache with others.

A couple months later a large group of us decided to finally tackle this enigma. No one in this group had managed to complete the cache, but a few had made varied levels of progress. We got to work and quickly discovered that this was going to be a massive undertaking with multiple stages and various techniques, and we LOVED it! There were about 10 of us working on it while the sole finders watched and laughed.

When we were finally able to open what we thought was the final container, we discovered not a logsheet as we had hoped, but a key with a tag. On one side of the tag were about 6 random letters and numbers, and on the other side was the cryptic hint, "Driver's side."

We all stopped and pondered for a moment. Then we realized we were standing next to a huge parking lot. None of us knew what else to try, so we started searching the lot, the previous finders chuckling to themselves.

We were ALL surprised when we heard, "GOT IT!" from a corner of the parking lot. Sure enough, here was a huge box truck with a license plate that matched the tag! The tires were flat and the license plates had expired years ago, but it was a definite match!

We tried the key on the driver's side, but it didn't fit. Someone else reached in through the open window on the passenger's side and opened the door. Another person checked the contents of the box portion of the truck. At one point we were so out of ideas I searched underneath the truck while another person climbed on top of it. It was now dark and we'd been searching everywhere we could think of for about an hour when a car pulled up, shining its lights on us.

"What are you doing in my truck?!" a man yelled from the car.

We all blankly looked at each other, trying to determine if this was the cache owner playing a trick or a legitimate problem. We tried explaining geocaching and what we were doing, but after a short time he accused us of stealing his property, locked himself in his car and rolled up his window, and called the police. He then moved his car into a position to block in one of our cars to prevent us from getting away.

We looked at the previous finders, who confirmed we were definitely in the right place for the cache. They were just as surprised as we were. A sweet older lady in our group tried to reason with the man in the car, but he wanted nothing to do with us until the police arrived.

Michael, the owner of the barricaded car, told everyone else to leave, and said that there was no reason for all of us to get questioned. We argued and said we were all doing this together, but he insisted, so we all spread out and returned to our cars.

As we were getting ready to leave, Michael had figured out a way to maneuver out of the "blockade" and was leaving the parking lot with the "truck owner" following closely behind him, angrily talking on his phone. The rest of us agreed to leave and meet up at a local establishment to figure out what to do next.

Meanwhile we were getting updates from Michael's wife. Michael was driving around the area at a leisurely pace while the truck owner was frantically weaving in and out of traffic to stay with him. When Michael realized this guy was not going to leave, he pulled into an abandoned Big Lots parking lot.

Suddenly his car was surrounded by police cruiser after police cruiser: 3, 4, 5... Michael's wife guessed around six but couldn't be certain with all of the flashing lights and confusion around their car. The spotlight from the police helicopter circling above the car was probably making it difficult, as well.

A police officer came up to the car and explained to Michael that the truck owner claimed they had been stealing from his box truck. Michael calmly told the officer that if he wanted, he could search his vehicle; the only thing he had was his wife and his young child in the car. The police officer made a cursory glance around the car, saw that Michael was telling the truth, and inexplicably told him that he was free to go.

Michael didn't wait around to ask questions. His family met us at the rendezvous point and told us everything that had happened. I still believe Michael had some sort of government connection and secret password that could get him out of ANY situation, but he always denied it with a twinkle in his eye.

Good Lock was taken down immediately due to a "lack of adequate owner permission."

Heh... ya think?!

Hot Adventure on Hot Wheels

Eric Coulombe

FrogMastr

This was a hot summer day in late August. But what a day! I woke up and felt that this day should be a day for a challenge, a hot challenge and a difficult challenge. The sky was clear and the temperature was high; the kind of day that that should have you outside in it. I woke the little family consisting of my girlfriend and my 9 year old son and packed the stuff for our geocaching day target: GCWNG1, 117 Hot wheels Kinojevis. (Canada)

I was at the beginning of my geocacher experience. I had at that time, about 100 or so finds. Just enough to know what the difficulty rating meant... And that should have prepared me for our little adventure. We started the van and went on the planned road trip with about 100 kilometers scheduled for the day. Had a couple stops on the way (of course every geocacher knows that the real average mileage of a geocacher is less than 20 kilometers per hour counting all the stops!) A couples of micros on the way, some bigger some awesome custom made containers with all different camoed types. We were all happy of the trip so far. Temperature was getting hot, very hot but great for a day of adventure.

After those successful smiling waypoints on the GPS we hit the destination: GCWNG1. The view was scenic; from the roadside we were able to see the cliff side. I would say about 100 to 150 meters deep, a straight drop, and about 2 to 5 kilometers long. Bare rocks with hardly any vegetation that was able to grow in that uncompromising landscape. At the bottom of the canyon (it seemed like a canyon to me!) was a river about 100 meters wide. Brown water flowing beside heavy and broken rocks; not the kind of river you want to take a plunge into!

The trailhead was at the top of the cliff. From there we could see the entire river under the bridge crossing the canyon. I felt so small beside that huge landscape. At that point I was looking at my GPS and the direction it was pointing in was directly at the cliff side. In that moment, I just had my first shivers. What were we getting into?

We proceed to cross the bridge and took the trail. About 150 meters along the trail, the GPS arrow was still going toward the cliff. As a responsible father and boyfriend I wanted my little family to stay safe. So I told them to stay on top of the ledge while I went a little further to investigate the area. About 25 meters later I was on the side of the cliff, hanging by my fingers on the face of the rocks. The ground was a slippery, maybe because of my sweat...

Did I mention the terrain rating on the cache was 4.5 stars? At that point I remembered that – and started wondering what I was doing there.

On the top of the escarpment, my girlfriend was asking me if everything was okay. Of course it was all okay – I was just hanging by roots to keep balance over a 100 meter drop and the stupid GPS telling me to go juuuuust a little farther, over there!

I yelled at her, "Do not come here! It's dangerous! Stay on top!"

Then I told her, "I'm almost there... about 12 meters to go!"

And I was still not able to see that darn cache. It was supposed to be a medium size so I SHOULD be able to see it at 10 meters away, right ? My progression was more and more scary... (By the way I have absolutely NO fear of heights... as far as I knew!)

Now only 3 meters to go so THAT should be the GZ spot, right? I could hear my son and girlfriend, asking me "Do you see it?"

"NO!" I yelled back. "But since I am here I WILL find it!!" I was not about to turn back empty handed for sure! One little step... falling rocks under my feet, my hand still gripping a small tree and wondering why it was suddenly so heavy. I can see my girlfriend from up above, looking back at me... And I'm thinking to myself, at least they are at a safe place,

She asked me again if she could help... "NO YOU CAN'T, STAY AWAY!"

Not in front, not at the back, not under my feet: WHERE COULD IT BE!!!

At that point I was about to accept my fate and log a painful DNF when I heard a friendly but "trolling" voice from above.... "Do you see that?"

There, IN her HANDS, a small thread going down...

She pulled on it...

And pulled...

And guess what? YUP! There it was! That "stupid" cache was just OVER my head! (The only place I hadn't looked, about 3 feet above my nose!)

She asked me if she should pull it up so we could get it and sign it. I said, "NO! I am here I will sign it FROM here!"

I signed the cache, hanging on to the cliff face with one hand...

Then they pulled it up to the top by the wire and signed it for themselves. Then let it go back in place hanging just above my face!

When I made it back to the top, safely reunited with my little family, I was a bit less grumpy! BUT, my blood was still pumping! Part adrenalin and part frustration but seeing them laughing made me feel better!

That was a Big Adventure but a great adventure! And I was proud of that 5/4.5 cache! We went back to the car and enjoyed the rest of our day! That is the kind of experiences that made me love geocaching.

The Challenging Geocache

Misty Mott

Misty's Shadow

The difficulty is three, the terrain is a two
The coordinates are calling out to you.
You know there's a hint but you cannot yet peek
For any clue to the cache you seek.

You quickly turn on your GPS
As to the direction, you dare not just guess.
The distance is fair, but not really far
A kilometer away, who needs a car?

Grab a trail map and pull on your pack,
The cache is calling now – don't look back!
Follow the blazes until you get near,
Then through the bushes it tells you to steer.

Over the rock wall and under the thorns,
The prickers and stickers you ever do scorn.
The GPS says its only meters ahead
You pick up the pace and duck your head.

That branch almost took off some of your hair
But you were quicker than a gust of fresh air.
You swerved and ducked, just in time
Then felt a rock like a turn on a dime.

Slowing down so you do not get hurt
You can't help but feel an energy spurt.
The cache is so close you know it's right here

And a DNF you ever do fear.

You lift and you look and you poke and you pry
Then finally the container in green do you spy.
You quickly open it and cry out with delight,
A nice dry logbook is right there in sight!.

Scanning the pages you see familiar names
Of all those cachers to this cache who came,
You sit quietly and add your own insight
Hearing the birds sing as you carefully you write.

Sealing it tightly, you re-hide the cache
Watching a Blue Jay ever so brash.
Reluctantly you turn for the walk to the car
Thinking it really was not so hard.

The sun is setting and getting quite low
As down the trail you hurry and go;
As you walk you can't help but say,
"Are there other caches along the way?"

Steel Fears

Kelly Rysten

Rysten

It's barely dawn. I stand looking at the structure before me. There's a micro cache on it. Somewhere. A homeless man rides by on an old bicycle, rags flapping, all his belongings in a little trailer that threatens to tip over with every bump. He looks my way and begins to smile, then the smile quickly fades and his eyes narrow. Shoot. Am I attracting attention already? I haven't even started looking yet! TSPI and I came to look for 'Steel Sphere' before downtown got busy, but there is no such thing as a quiet morning in downtown Lancaster.

We walk up to the sphere. Yes, it's a big steel sphere on the main drag. It looks like it's made from I-beams but they are bent to form a sphere. There aren't many hiding places. Everything is very open. I don't want to touch the electrical box but I can see it does open. I sure don't want to open it though. It looks like it shouldn't be messed with.

A police car glides by and I suddenly quit looking at the electrical box. *Just what we need*, I think, *a geocaching lesson with an officer of the law.* The car keeps going and I breathe a sigh of relief, only to see an older couple walking down The Boulevard hand in hand. I consult my GPS even though I know I'm standing at ground zero.

An old man walks up and I greet him with a, "Good morning." He seems to notice we are looking for something so he gets a short geocaching explanation.

"I used to do that," he said. "Them geodes sure are pretty when you break 'em open."

There is no way we would find a geode on a paved sidewalk but he seems content that he's got us pegged as geode hunters. I let him think we are just lousy rock hounds.

The cache was very popular, a sneaky hide that the geocaching community seemed very proud of. Then a string of DNFs darkened its history and locals began giving up on ever finding it. Just like us, many people had looked for it several times with no luck. But recently our friends,

SnoopyRocks and Palmdalepea, found it so we knew it was there! They even posted pictures! We want to help this cache find a place on the geocaching map again so we are very determined to find it too.

Every person who walks by causes me to stiffen and change my search tactics, which I'm sure just makes me look even more suspicious. Maybe we should give up again.

Even though it is still early, an employee at the nearby restaurant comes to get the business ready for the lunch crowd. I remember that a waitress in the restaurant still questioned the cache's existence. Well, if we find it she still wouldn't see it. It's too early for her to show up at work. The employee turns and I wonder if he's going to question our activities, but he just pauses and then goes inside.

I run my fingers over every reachable crevice I can see and behind some things where I can't see. Surely the cache is hidden out of sight behind a little utility box, or behind the conduit running up the I-beam. Nope.

The longer I look for the cache the more the muggles around us appear to be pausing and mentally questioning our movements. And the more I question their thoughts the more I worry about my actions. I'm entering a downward spiral that can only be eased by either giving up or finding the cache. But we just have to find it this time! We're tired of DNFing this one cache.

A lady walks by with three little dogs. Two of the dogs happily trot beside their owner but the white fluffy one stops and looks like it wants to break the tempo of the walk. *No, Fido,* I think, *just keep walking. We don't need a tangle of leashes right at ground zero. Heel! Good boy.*

Another police car. I remind myself the station is only a few blocks away. They don't really have the whole squad cruising past because of us. They're just going to the station. The sun is rising and more people will be showing up soon. Maybe we should go home and come back earlier another morning. We had arrived at dawn. We can't begin much earlier. Okay, one more feel. I'm convinced I won't see the cache. If I could see it the cache would have been found already.

TSPI and I switch off repeatedly. I search the lower, street side of the sphere while TSPI searches the upper, inside part. When one of us gives up, we switch. Back and forth, back and forth. Then suddenly he walks around to the front of the sphere again. I thought he was going to switch positions again but he opens his hand. A nano! Yes! Finally! We found it!

We take pictures to prove we really found Steel Sphere.

This doesn't sound like much of an adventure except that the intensity of every thought was magnified by a hundred. You see, every day I deal with an affliction that will never go away. Thanks to a patient husband who helps me work my way through it, I pretty much keep agoraphobia at bay. It takes a lot of exposure to muggles to make me see that the real world is not a fearful place. Geocaching helps keep my focus on a task instead of on my fear. If I let my fears win I become a hermit, living contentedly in my house. Geocaching opens up the world for me, and it's a tool I enjoy using on a regular basis. Maybe people do see me as strange when I geocache, but that's okay.

Snoopy Rocks and Palmdalepea's find encouraged us to look again for Steel Sphere and our find backed up theirs, which sparked a long string of new finds. We are glad to see it back on the radar of the local geocachers. Many of the logs, just like ours, contain the word finally!

Go geocaching. See the world.

Cache-22

LeeAnn Bachman

penguins188

A sharp whistle split the air as a text notification came through on my cell phone. A new geocache was published!

"Looks like it's on a trail," I thought. "A little over eight miles. I should wait until they're all published before I head out."

After doing a little research on geocaching.com, I realized the caches were on the new trail we were planning on placing a few caches on. We had driven by the trailhead a few times and it looked promising.

It was a few hours after doing some work around the house when we decided it was about time to head out for the new geocaches, even though we knew that by that time we had no chance of being first to find.

I turned on my GPS and hit the "Find Nearest" button on the geocaching app on my phone. The first cache was only a few feet from the trailhead. It wasn't a recently published one, but it was still fairly new, and we hadn't found it yet.

It didn't take long to realize this cache might take a little while to find. Wanting to find the new ones, we didn't spend too much time searching. We let a family on mountain bikes pass before we set back out on the trail.

As we were approaching ground zero of the first new cache, we saw the family on their bikes that had just passed by us when we were searching for the other cache up by the trailhead. The family seemed to be slowing down near the location of where my GPS said the cache was.

Were they geocachers, or would we have to wait out some resting muggles? We had our answer when GPS units appeared and the adults jumped off their bikes just as fast, or perhaps even faster, than their children.

"Are you geocachers?" my mother asked the family, now trampling the ferns and getting stuck in the gooey mud next to a fallen, rotting tree trunk covered in woodpecker holes.

"Yeah," the mother replied, and told us their geocaching name. They shared one geocaching name as a family, just like us. They found the cache first, while straddling a huge fallen tree trunk.

When we were about five-hundred feet away from the cache, the trees started thinning to give way to houses, and eventually a fence-lined, carless road. Houses appeared after the road, with the first one far back into the brush and small enough to be a large garage. Next to it and much closer to the trail was a medium sized house with a large pond out front. A newer wooden fence wrapped around the perimeter of the house. A man was mowing his lawn with a riding mower up by the house, but didn't seem to notice us. He was far enough away that you could barely hear his mower from the trail.

We reached a point where the ground dipped slightly away from the trail. It was a small clearing, probably about six feet long by three feet wide. At the far end of the clearing was a dead tree covered in moss and lichen. It seemed several generations of insects have enjoyed the tasty feast for many years, as it was more of a huge pile of rotted bark than a fallen tree. It was amazing the thing was still suspended by a rock and the other end of itself that had snapped off. We grabbed the cache hidden in the tree, signed the log, and just as we were replacing it, the mother of the other geocaching team declared, "It looks like we have company." We quickly replaced the cache, expecting other geocachers.

Just as we're emerging from the brush, the man we noticed mowing his grass up by the house pulled up alongside the other side of the fence. Anyone would be able to tell by the look of his face that he was absolutely fuming. Then suddenly, he was screaming at us, declaring that he had to chase two other people out of there that day, that it was private property, we had no business there, and what did we think we were doing in there anyway?

The mother of the other geocaching team did all of the talking for everyone.

"I'm sorry if we bothered you, sir, but we're geo-" she tried to explain before she was cut off.

He started yelling again about chasing people out of there and began demanding to see the container. He announced to the whole world he would take it.

As a counter-attack, the mother, biting her tongue, told him, "Sir, I don't see any Private Property signs. It's park property, so we're allowed to be here."

He wasn't taking any of it. He even threatened to call the police on us! At that point he started getting out of the seat of his lawnmower and we didn't want to find out what he was going to do. We all decided it was time to just keep moving and let Mr. Irate-Lawnmower-Man burn off his anger and finish mowing his grass before someone got hurt unnecessarily.

"Go ahead and call the cops then. Just do it. We weren't hurting anyone," the father of the other family told the man as we all started walking away. I just wanted to get out of there.

As soon as we arrived home, I turned on the computer and logging in the caches we found. There were already a few logs mentioning Lawnmower-Man. Turns out, Lawnmower-Man actually did call the police and even had the nerve to follow the other cacher back to the second cache!

But me – I love geocaching so much that this one instance isn't going to make me stop caching!

Fall in the Creek

Tim Martin

Rubicon Cacher

Where to begin...

I guess I'll begin this unforgettable experience with the Difficulty 3.5/Terrain 4.0 rating of the cache. I'd been watching this cache (GC9E6A) for some time hoping it would be reactivated because I need the D/T rating to complete another of the 81 D/T combinations for the "Well Rounded Cacher" challenge. I was getting close and this cache was perfect to help me reach my goal. After I saw that the cache had been reactivated, I planned our weekend geocaching trip to get this one off my "to do" list.

Mistake #1

The GPS says it's only a little over 400 feet from the parking area. I figure that I don't need my hiking shoes so off I go wearing my Crocs.

Mistake #2

I really should go up and around that muddy, washed out area close to the water but it's only a couple of feet across – so no problem.

Mistake #3

I didn't watch my foot placement very well and stepped on a slight down-sloped area that was very muddy and only about 1.5 feet from the water's edge.

What was the result of these mistakes? You guessed it! I slipped in the mud because I was too close to the edge, wearing improper footwear, and being careless!

I take a dive into Big Bear Creek. At the point of my 0.1 rated dive into the water, the bank slopes sharply and I went in neck deep and felt myself slipping even further into the very cold water. My feet were slipping and sliding on the bottom... I'm not a very good swimmer, especially fully dressed. Uh-oh!

I finally got close to the bank and was able to grab a submerged root or something that was sturdy enough to help me get out of the water. That's when I realized that my GPS was gone. Yes, the Delorme PN-40 SE is waterproof but it doesn't float. So, rather than get out of the water, I felt around the creek bottom as far out and as deep as I could – while still holding on to the root.

I stayed in the cold water feeling around for my GPS until hypothermia started to set in. Unfortunately for me, some lucky fish is now using my GPS to navigate the waters of Big Bear Creek.

After I started turning blue I decided to give up on my fruitless search. I was saturated from my feet to my chin - fortunately, my head never went under the water. Brrrrr!

By this time, I was really starting to feel the cold and was shivering badly. I knew that I needed to get out of the soaked clothes as quickly as possible. Fortunately, Lady Gem - my bride of thirty-five years - and I had planned a Friday and Saturday caching run, so we had our packed suitcase in the Jeep. Luckily, no one else was around but it really wouldn't have mattered to me at that point because I had to get dry. So, I stripped down to my birthday suit and dried myself using one of the towels that we always carry with us and then put on dry clothes. Lady Gem had started the engine and warmed up the Jeep so I climbed in for a few minutes to warm myself while putting on my hiking shoes.

I just had to get that D3.5/T4.0 cache especially after the steep price I paid for it! I would have stayed until dark had it been necessary to find the cache! So, I got out my Garmin Colorado which, because while I like (liked!) the Delorme better, the Garmin had become my backup GPS.

Lady Gem and I headed back toward the cache site. We took the same route but because I now wore my hiking shoes and really watched my footing, we made it across the washed out area without problem. After a few minutes of searching, Lady Gem spotted a likely place and, sure enough, there was the cache!

I had been carrying my trade items in my geocaching bag when I fell in earlier so the bag and all of the contents were as saturated as I was so I had nothing to trade but I took a pocket knife anyway. I signed the log for both of us and we headed back to the Jeep.

On the way back to the Jeep, we used the higher ground and circled around the washed out and very slippery area. The bushwhacking was much better than my very cold and unplanned swim!

Stories of Connection

Ode to Swamp Rats

Mimi Barrison
M&M Melted

Nessie swims that Scottish loch,
in the woods the Skunk Ape stalks.
Count Dracula becomes a bat,
but wherefore dwells The Rat?

"EEK!" you scream,
"A rat, pray tell,
why speak you of that beast?
call an exterminator,
keep it away!
Not legendary, no way!"

Fear not, good friend,
this Rat is not
the rodent you fear.
A brand of geocacher
so strange and rare –
our story hear!

Floridians one and all we are,
with Geocaching in our blood,
we meet and seek and reveal
where the waters like to flood.

"Why swamps?" you ask
"Isn't where reptilian beasties reside?
There be geocaches everywhere…why risk your hides?"

Well swamps are sites of beauty
with flora and fauna to spare
mega cypress trunks to hug
and greenery everywhere.

Alligators? Yes indeed!
so common sense prevails.
We wade where feet can touch the ground
and not where a gator sails.

"And what about those slithering snakes?
Do they not pose a threat?
The cottonmouths & rattlers?
They must be there, I bet!"

Swamp Rats, adventurers are we,
but also we take the time
to keep our eyes wide open
and avoid the snakely slime.

But don't get us wrong, my friend,
these creatures have their place
and Swamp Rats love to see them –
of course from a safe space!

So parking lots abandoned.
Guardrail micros left behind.
In the wetlands of Central Florida
festive Swamp Rats you will find.

A Quick Stop Along the Way

Andrea Tantillo

tantillos.com

My dad didn't understand why our drive from Houston, Texas, to Smackover, Arkansas, was taking 8 or 9 hours instead of the usual 7.

"You're just looking for boxes and putting them back? You don't even get to keep them? Why don't you just skip that nonsense and get on up here to see your daddy." That was his mantra.

And we could understand why he didn't get it. He'd never experienced the thrill of the hunt. He didn't know what it was like to stealthily lift a light pole skirt and act like nothing unusual is happening when that film canister rolls out. He didn't know the sheer terror you feel, followed by the utter relief when you think you hear something large in the bushes – and it turns out to be a squirrel. He didn't know what it felt like to walk through the woods for what seems like hours hot, dirty, scraped up, and frustrated by not finding the holy grail (ammo can) and then hearing that beautiful "ka-thunk" when finally you poke your stick in the right pile of pine straw and find the prize.

So, after two or three trips home to visit my dad, listening to him fuss about us playing our silly little game and delaying our visits with him, my husband and I figured we should take an afternoon to show him what it was all about. In 2006, there were only 2 active geocaches within a 30-mile radius of my dad's house - one in town in front of the Chamber of Commerce building and one in the neighboring town just outside of an old cemetery. The three of us quickly found those two, and then drove to north Louisiana to find a few more. That trip came up a little empty, as geocaching trips will do sometimes. We only found one and never could figure out how to navigate around a large lake to ground zero to even look for a second cache. Dad thought the game was interesting, but still a little silly.

So, we kept coming for visits and he kept scolding us for wasting time getting there. We had no intention of not geocaching, but still I was feeling a little guilty making him wait for our arrival. Especially since I knew if he could ever get a real taste for geocaching, he'd want us to stop and find some along the way. And I was right about that.

Thanks to a rainy fall weekend and a ton of caches hidden around the Angelina National Forest placed by The Pastor & Pastor's Wife in northeast Texas, my dad was finally hooked. We must have found over 50 caches that weekend. Dad was slow at first, but by the end of the weekend, his poking stick was "ka-thunking" more than mine. That trip also struck a chord that I didn't expect from him. Sometime during the middle of that trip he realized that even though there weren't any caches around his house for him to find, there was nothing stopping him from hiding some of his own around the area for other people.

My dad grew up in south Arkansas and worked in the oil fields in for years. He knows a lot of people who were more than happy to let him hide a cache or two on their property, just off an old oil field road, over there by the cow pasture, or right up in the middle of town beside the grocery store.

In a single month in 2008 my dad, allernearl58, hid 67 caches within a 30-mile radius of his house. That amount of FTFs in a concentrated area caught the attention of a few seasoned cachers from north and central Arkansas (where caches were not nearly as sparse). They made the trip down, got in touch with my dad, and took him along with them while they found every one of his caches. Geocachers rklmbl and woodwalker9 spent the entire day with my dad, giving him pointers and encouraging him to keep up the good work. Before they left, they hid 10 caches in the area so my dad would have some to look for too.

Over the next year, more and more cachers visited the area from other parts of the state, other states, and even other towns in south Arkansas, just to find allenearl58's caches. And pretty soon, some of those new south Arkansas cachers began to hide caches of their own. The area really took off as a hotbed for geocaching - so much so that Groundspeak even brought their travelling Official Geocaching GPS Maze Exhibit to a state park museum in Smackover in 2009.

My dad also scheduled the first Fired Up for Geocaching (GC303EP) event that year, which drew visitors from 6 states (though most of the credit for the success of that event lies with the proximity to the Groundspeak exhibit.) The Fired Up for Geocaching event is still ongoing in Smackover each summer, with at least 50 participants turning out to enjoy the day.

Today, there are more than 1,000 active geocaches hidden within a 30-mile radius of my dad's house. Every visit to south Arkansas includes at least one day of geocaching, sometimes more. And now he asks how many caches we found on our way up from Houston, Texas, to Smackover, Arkansas. And 9 hours seems like making good time these days.

Beauty in Abandonment

Marie Kolibas

Divine Amorphis

When I first heard about geocaching in 2008, I wanted nothing to do with it. It was a beautiful summer day and my best friend and I had taken the bike up the mountain to one of my favorite places, a cluster of abandoned houses in Tranquility, New Jersey.

It was a place we had been several times, a place I found peaceful and beautiful in its own decaying way. We started with the houses down below and then headed up to the mansion. He went out back to "use the bathroom" and I headed up to the attic. I had just started to take photos when he called me to come downstairs. Apparently while kicking over things in the area to see what was there, he found something that didn't seem to belong with the rest of the rubbish. As we were examining it, two guys came running up saying "Oh, you found it."

They gave us a brief explanation and I remember saying "There is an abandoned mansion behind us and you want me to pay attention to a container in the woods!" So I left, went back into the house, and promptly forgot about geocaching.

Three years later I lost that friend. Nothing was the same; I felt like I never said goodbye. I never left the house; my camera sat unused collecting layers of dust. I took down all the photos I had framed around the house, pulled all of my work from the local gallery in which it was displayed. My relationship failed and I couldn't keep friends. My life became work, kids, and sleep. The only reminder of that part of my life was a key we found in one of the abandoned houses. I wore it constantly.

Then, in 2012 while on vacation with my family, a friend mentioned that he was going to get a geocache. I nearly broke an ankle trying to get off my lounge chair. My first cache was a bison in a tree. Nothing exciting. I couldn't even tell you the name, but caching was the activity those two guys had been talking about all those years before.

I wanted to go back to that first accidental cache, to see it one more time, to say goodbye to my friend. I wanted closure. I had no idea how I would find the exact area again or if the cache was still active. But I knew I was going to try and find it.

Caching became a sort of savior to me. I stopped hating mornings, started to leave the house more. I looked forward to weekends and adventures. After a while, I dusted off the camera. I even was able to start making friends again.

After several caching adventures, my numbers started to climb. We did everything from power trails, to tree climbs, and paddling hides. I attended dozens of events and went on several road trips. There was really no preference to what we did. What mattered was I was having fun. Soon everyone was asking about what I was going to do for the big 1,000 find milestone.

Suggestions came in from everyone. They ranged from caches that were popular, to ones that were more my style. But none felt right.

Even after selecting a cache, I kept looking at a cache I had bookmarked the first month I started caching. A simple cache, a few feet off the trail, no swag, no special camo, the owner was not even active any more. Not a lot of people were finding it, and there was no promise it was still even there. But to me, it was special and had meaning.

On the advice of others, I continued to make plans to go out of state for a series of great caches, even though doing so felt half-hearted. Then, it snowed. Not just a dusting, but several feet of snow – to the point that our plans had to be canceled. And that was when I knew; I was going to that cache, the one with so much meaning to me. The cache was simple, even bordering on boring. But it was at that abandoned house; the one where I had first learned about geocaching.

On the snowy morning of January 19th, 2014, six geo-buddies and I took the trek up to Allamuchy State Forest. We ran through the houses, taking photos and laughing. Eventually we remembered what we were there for and found the cache before enjoying more play time.

Although the original cache I had "found" a few years ago was no longer there, being back at that house was such an amazing experience. So much I remembered from the previous times I was there, but yet there were still new things to see. The place was falling apart; graffiti everywhere, holes in the floor, peeling wall paper. Yet, it was perfect. I didn't even cry. I had a new hobby, new friends and a new outlook on life. Geocaching was the start of a new beginning, and I love it more and more each day.

A Renewed Connection

Kellie Parker

Kelhparker

I have a boy-child on the cusp of teenage years. It's tricky. He's in that in between stage. Not a little kid anymore and not yet a teenager, but instead… somewhere stuck in the middle, in no man's land. He still love games, but is loath to admit it because it's just so not cool. I can tell he feels the pressure from his peers to act a certain way and to like certain things and to not like other things anymore.

And what about me as a parent? The hugs are still there, if a little half-hearted, especially when his mates are around. He thinks he has more answers to life's questions than I do, because I'm 'Out Of Touch' and 'Have No Idea'. *(Regardless of my constant reminders I've been on this earth 28 years longer than him!)*

He is now officially taller than me and bigger than me and thinks it's entertaining to come up behind me and scoop me off the ground, because you know, he can.

There is a definite shift in the way he sees me. The respect and love are still there, I can see that, and still feel that, but the relationship is shifting. It's scary. As much as I desperately want to hold on to my little boy, I am also excited to get to know this new version of him that is evolving.

I want to keep the connection between us alive. It needs to evolve with him as he changes so that he still enjoys spending time with me.

How can I, without forcing it? How do I get him away from the iPod for a minute to get a decent conversation? How do I get him to engage with his younger sister without the bribery? How do get him off the couch, off social media?

Enter… geocaching. What a wonderful discovery!

I came across it purely by chance and uncovered a *Whole New World*. It seemed to be huge. How exciting to think that there were hidden treasures all over the world - millions of them - that I had no idea about. But surely there wouldn't be any in this part of the world, little old Tasmania Australia?

How wrong I was!

There are heaps, and not only that, some, are just around the corner. When I mentioned it to my son he was instantly hooked. He took over the coordinates and I packed us a bag, and off we went.

I had a list of about 5 caches we could hunt for that day (foolishly I thought they would be super easy to find) and we set off with our little 4 year old Chief Treasure Hunter, my daughter, in tow.

We picked a great day to find our first one, we had no *real* idea what we were doing, so it was handy that the city of Hobart is rather sleepy on a Sunday and so we were not observed behaving strangely by too many muggles (My son nearly flipped when he heard that non-geocachers were referred to as Muggles).

We had the coordinates, we could tell we were getting close, but where was it? We had been at this for two hours... (Yes, I know, I know, but remember, we are novices here)

"Let's call it a day and come back another time," I said, thinking the kids were getting bored and that perhaps this was a bit of a dud adventure.

"No way!" My son said. "Wait here."

I watched him as he causally walked past a muggle and then sprinted, as soon as he was out of sight, hunched over like some sort of action hero in a spy movie avoiding bullets. He ran down the tunnel and out of sight, where it went under the street, and then came up the other side of the road, where he casually leaned against the railing, trying to look like he had not a care in the world whilst surreptitiously running his hands underneath the pole.

In an instant his face changed. One minute he's Mr. Cool and the next, he's full of elation as he ripped his arm out and waved the cache in the air.

"IT'S THE TREASURE! I WANT THE TREASURE!" My 4 year old yelled for all the muggles to hear. (Thankfully there were none around!) I grabbed her hand and we ran together through the tunnel and up the other side to the hero of the day.

It was the tiniest thing I have ever seen. No room to put our name on the log, but we felt so proud of ourselves.

We beamed at each other. What a strange sight we would have made, the three of us in a circle all looking in wonder at this tiny object, trying to be cool about it but failing miserably.

We each took turns to touch it and marvel at finding our very first 'Treasure'. We were officially a part of the club. We carefully put it back, looking over our shoulder to make sure we were alone.

And we were done. We were also exhausted.

We decided to leave the other four for another day and instead headed to a café where we had cake and hot chocolate and reveled in our success, feeling rather proud of ourselves.

What a great day! What a great connection to remake with my son!

What a great hobby to have, one that mixes math, exercise, and adventure and best of all… it's free. It was one of the best afternoons I have had with my son in a long time. We made a connection. We had something that was just for us (and the Chief Treasure Hunter, of course.)

On the drive home, my son, busily plotted our next adventure.

The Quest Starts Here

Amy Zellmer

flamingoamyjo

It was a beautiful July evening in Saint Paul, Minnesota. My friend, Bruce, had stopped by on his motorcycle to hang out. We had just finished going for a walk around my building and were sitting outside enjoying the warm breeze and taking in the moonlight.

Bruce pulled out his iPhone and commented that there must be some geocaches nearby. I had heard of geocaching before, but had never participated in it and actually thought it sounded boring. Once he opened the app and read the hint, I was intrigued. I had no idea there would be CLUES, a scavenger hunt of sorts. I had envisioned coordinates and a compass, like what I had done in elementary school; and could never find my target. Now this, this sounded like it could be fun! Armed with our cellphone flashlights, we began our quest.

At the time Bruce was an over-the-road bus driver, and would take tours of people across the US. During his down-time he would search for caches in his area to pass the time.

Based on the first hint we were given, I thought knew right where it was. Or should be. We searched for about 15 minutes and couldn't find it. That'll teach me to think I can geocache without a GPS!

Bruce eventually pulled up the cache page on his phone and realized that for the past few months no one had been able to find it.

We moved onto the next cache, again, I thought I knew right where it was from the hint. Bruce found it with little effort. I thought, *Okay, this is kinda fun. Not at all like what I remember from scavenger hunts from elementary school!*

I was instantly addicted. There was a third cache nearby and I begged Bruce to go find it, even though he was ready to head home to bed. He finally relented...I It WAS a gorgeous night to be outside after all!

I knew where the GPS was leading us and began investigating a sign on the street behind my building, off of the sidewalk. Bruce told me that the caches should always be hidden in a safe place, which led me to believe it was hidden in the sign. Being a newbie, I didn't realize I needed to poke my fingers behind where the post attaches behind the sign. I gave up my search and moved over to where Bruce was fishing around. He commented that he didn't have his "tool kit" with him, which made me giggle. He told me this was a serious sport, and detailed some of the items in his tool kit: magnet, mirror on a stick, tape, paper, pen, etc. I had no clue geocachers took their finds so seriously!

After not finding it where he was looking, he moved over to the sign I had just investigated. He shoved his finger up behind the post and voila! There it was. It had been right under my nose the entire time.

"Rookie mistake," he told me. We had a good laugh that it had been exactly where I was looking, I just didn't look hard enough. In all fairness, I was afraid to poke my finger into a hole and find a spider!

After our third find Bruce ventured home and I went into my loft and downloaded the free app to my phone to see what other treasures were lurking in my area. I texted him and told him we need to head over to Harriet Island, there appeared to be a whole collection of geocaches there. He laughed and said he was glad I had fun, and that he had opened my eyes to a new hobby.

Just like Bruce, I've started geocaching when I am on road trips. It opens me up to new places I never would have seen!

I am glad he was able to open my eyes to an exciting and fun new pastime that gorgeous July evening!

Thanks For The Cache

Emily Albers
Stardust2018

Some found a cache,
Picked up some trash.
There were muggles around,
But what was hidden, stayed sound.
Thanks for the cache!

Some logged a Did Not Find,
Those didn't set us behind.
There sat a trackable bug,
In the cache, all nice and snug.
Thanks for the cache!

Some swag we took;
Put some in the nook.
There we had a First To Find,
Celebrated it, tongue-tied.
Thanks for the cache!

Buckskin Run's Last Geocache

Jami Lewis

Sidekick of *Buckskin Run*

"May your trails be crooked, winding, lonesome, dangerous, leading to the most amazing view. May your mountains rise into and above the clouds." - Edward Abbey

Normally, I wouldn't dream of blessing someone with such a statement! Crooked? Dangerous? Who wishes such things for another? Yet life is full of twists and turns and loneliness, and eventually we do experience all, or almost all, of them. And many of life's challenges do lead to those amazing views.

That's how it was for us on one particularly special geocaching adventure. After two years of cancer treatments and all the hardship that goes along with it, my husband, Doug – also known as Buckskin Run in the geocache universe – was weary, but excited for a weekend getaway with our hiking, backpacking, and geocaching buddies, Ed and Cindy. Doug had not been feeling well for months, but he didn't whine or complain. After all, he had beat cancer 17 years ago, and all indications were that he would do so again.

The first leg of our journey involved a bit of time traveling – where the "new" art of geocaching met the "old" along Arizona's Historic Route 66. It was a perfect Northern Arizona fall day, not hot, not cold, and only slightly breezy (not the usual hair-stripping wind!) The high desert's crisp blue sky and sporadic bursts of fall color tantalized the adventurer with more surprises to come. Turning off I-40 onto Route 66 in Seligman, we chugged out of 2013 and into another time and place. We eagerly anticipated searching for newly hidden treasures along one of the last intact sections of the iconic road we only knew about from textbooks, movies, or our parents' and grandparents' tall tales.

We pulled over to the first entry on the GPS and readied our gear – Doug and Cindy held the GPSs like Geiger counters, reaching out to lead us to the hidden treasures; Eddie held cache opening tools, should they be needed; I pocketed a couple pens to enter our visits on the caches' registry; and four cameras went along for the ride. Rather than racing in trying to be the first of the group to find the cache, on sudden impulse, I hung back, snapping pictures – compelled to capture my husband immersed in the experience.

Those caches pulled us right into the past as well as onto Edward Abbey's *'crooked, winding, lonesome, and dangerous'* trails. Most of the trails were benign, hidden in or near artifacts of the more recent past, as well as some that were millennia old. We dug up caches (spoiler alert!) in an ore car, beneath a dinosaur's shadow, in the view of a mesa and a Route 66 "town" made famous in a kids' animated movie (can you guess which one?), in museums and gift shops, and behind historic roadside stands.

We found a crooked trail near an ancient cavern, a winding trail along railroad tracks, and a bit of danger on top of a rock tower. I snapped a memorable picture of Doug on top of the tower, grinning broadly and holding the large cache aloft, like an athlete thrusting his series trophy into the air for all to admire. Like the surrounding historic landscape, that grin swept me back to younger days.

Then there was lonesome. We experienced that in the quiet stretches between museums, antique stores, historical markers, and other geocache sites. We found it on top of that rock tower after returning the cache, gazing down at the railroad tracks that wound in and around the hills and mesas and out over the high desert, unpunctuated by civilization, the breeze whispering of the emptiness of that land.

I glanced over at Doug as he stared out. Was he comparing those winding tracks to the twists and turns his life had taken? Was he wondering if there were yet more crooked and dangerous roads in his future? Or was he simply reveling in the creation and his place in it? Or both?

After more than half a day, we logged in our last cache, drove to the end of Route 66 and turned back onto the I-40 in Kingman. We all agreed: this had been one of our most memorable adventures together.

It was also to be our last.

Yes, Doug would have more of Edward Abbey's trails to follow, but that day, we all experienced most amazing views and during those hours, the specter of illness fell off Doug and he was his usual laughing, adventurous, and intensely curious self.

Months later, as I looked at the photographs of that adventure through my tears of grief, I stopped at the final one and caught my breath: It was taken from the car as we topped the hill leading out of Kingman, heading west. The road, devoid of buildings or vegetation, stretched away and up in the far distance to an unseen mountain pass. Likewise, Doug had been on the final stretch of his journey here on earth, preparing for Abbey's far off place where the mountain he was going to would rise into and above the clouds. As he did with all ventures, he settled in and prepared to meet it head on.

Operation: Failure

Elayna Barrison

Daughter of *M&M Melted*

I called it *Operation: Ellis Island.*

It failed.

After pretending to be in steerage for weeks in Mrs. Moskowitz's class, my parents decided to ignore my travel demands and instead decided to try a treasure hunt game called geocaching. As usual, I huffed my grievances, but they only went into a corner of my parents' minds known as "Elayna's Problems", never really to be addressed again. I pictured a simple game where we would enter a park – I pictured child's playground with bike paths – and a map upon entry. We'd follow the map until we came across a fallen tree that people had signed with a sharpie, and inside it, there'd be a treasure box filled with wonders. But I still really wanted to go to Ellis Island instead.

So I sat in the back seat of the car, pouting to myself over my lost cause, as we drove to a nearby park. What we came to did not have a swing set or a slide, to my disappointment, but instead there was a single path leading into the woods. My dad took out his little yellow GPS and turned it on with a beep. On the screen appeared a compass pointing us down the trail. My parents, my brother, and I walked down the trail together. I avoided what would occasionally become my "stomp and walk" where I would trail behind them just because I didn't want to be there.

My brother had the same wonderful trait, but that day, after getting over the initial disappointment of *Operation: Ellis Island's* failure, my attention fell onto the path before me. Honestly, that first geocaching path we walked on looked like any other wooded area on the north end of Long Island, New York. In all shapes and forms, the park was not one I'd even thought much about, but then again, when I was young when I thought about a park, I pictured a place with swing sets and a twisted slide. But according to that little yellow GPS, that's where this "treasure chest" in the woods waited to be found.

I don't think the walk was as long as it felt. But at four feet tall, a half mile felt like forever. If I had gone to Ellis Island, it would have been a train ride followed by a boat! Instead, I was walking on a trail that could have been the exercise trail near the public library. My mind didn't dwindle on my obsolete Operation Ellis Island much longer, however, since we eventually came to a wall of shrubs and trees. My dad told me that the treasure chest hid in there, and that we had to go find it. *Like hide 'n seek*, I thought! *Or I-Spy!*

I believe my dad was the one who finally found it, hiding under a small log right off the trail. It wasn't a special log with a giant red "X" on it, but a normal fallen tree, and beneath it lay a plastic container holding a memo pad - so that's what my parent's meant by "log" (not a fallen tree that people signed with a Sharpie).

And, to my excitement, TOYS! Free toys, like the ones at McDonald's or the Dollar Store! My mom told me that as long as we exchange something, I could get a toy! Okay, sure, I missed out on Operation: Ellis Island… but this was even better.

The walk back to the car felt shorter, as they usually do. At the time, my mind focused only on the goodies that waited in the treasure chest we would find next, and I don't think the other adventures even crossed my mind at the time…

How would I have known that geocaching would get my family lost in the woods, or take us up to Ithaca, New York to see the waterfalls? Could I have imagined those stone steps in New Jersey that George Washington supposedly used or the swamps we would discover after we moved to Florida? They didn't even cross my mind.

That was twelve years ago, and now I am nearly twenty-one. Geocaching has become a cornerstone of not only my life, but of the relationship I have with my parents. Although I definitely went through the "hermit" teenage years, coated with endless hours of staring at the computer monitor and hiding in my room, I never resented my parents in any way, shape, or form. Geocaching brought us back to the basics, where we could travel and see new things, like a natural swamp after walking into it knee deep in mud, or experience our wildest fears, like losing my brother in the woods – and after we found him, naming a cache "Where's Waldo?" – or running into a five-foot long pygmy rattlesnake. In the end, despite my eight-year-old-self dancing wildly over toys, or the talk of number counts piling sky high, what geocaching gave me was love.

I love nature, and though I do not cache under my own name, I find myself every weekend finding the natural nooks and crannies of Gainesville, Florida, where I am based now. I've been not only to Devil's Millhopper, but to other sink holes and out on the prairies where I can say, "Hey, this is the world we live for". And I love my family and what life has in store, all because of the world geocaching has opened my eyes.

So *Operation: Ellis Island* failed, but I cannot imagine how different my life would be if my parents had decided to listen to me.

An Obsession is Born

Jennifer Colgrove

jecolgrove

I was married for a little over two years, but the marriage was full of strife and unhappiness. When it ended, instead of feeling regret or loss I was overcome with relief. I had regained my autonomy. I felt free in a way that is almost impossible to explain, but because I had felt restrained for so long, I didn't believe I would ever again feel the need to enter into another partnership. Perhaps if I hadn't come across Andrew, I'd still feel that way.

Andrew and I have been dating for close to three years now. We've been together one year longer than I was married and I still feel tingly when I look at him. That may sound like a small thing, but after being subjected to negativity for such an extended period of time, it feels more like a deep stretch or the satisfaction one experiences after eating a delicious meal. Every moment I'm with him I feel energized. He has a fourteen year old son, Andy whom I adore, and who I get along with better than I could have ever dreamed possible. When the three of us hang out we have a blast; life is simply easy and enjoyable.

Andrew and I like to stay active; we enjoy going to concerts, taking random road trips, trying new restaurants, and taking photographs. On the weekends when Andy is with us, he happily accompanies us on all our adventures. Every now and then we run out of things to do and one of us will suggest something new. One particularly gloomy Saturday, when it seemed we were out of ideas, Andrew suggested we try geocaching. Andy and I had never heard of it before. Andrew explained that when he was younger, he and his mom and stepdad would geocache together. He spoke of day-long adventures that would take them into the woods, along the shores of Lake Erie and to hidden places he never knew existed. While he was explaining caching, all I could think was that it sounded like a treasure hunt. I could tell Andy was thinking the same thing. We were sold.

Despite our eagerness, our first geocaching endeavor did not start out well. We attempted to find a cache on a local college campus and failed. Next, we tried a historic church. Determined to be successful we searched the grounds for well over an hour and finally had to concede. Two DNF's in a row; a favorable outcome was seemingly beyond our grasp.

As if taking a cue from our moods, the weather began to turn. The sky started to cloud over, we could hear thunder rumbling in the distance and the humidity was off the charts. I was becoming discouraged, Andy was beginning to look bored, and Andrew was frustrated. Despite Mother Nature 's negative attitude and in spite of our growing despondency, we collectively selected our next attempt: a cache hidden within Penitentiary Glen, one of the Metroparks in the area. Andrew and I both tried to feign enthusiasm for Andy's sake, but it was clear if we didn't find this cache, it would be our first and last geocaching adventure.

One of the reasons we selected Penitentiary Glen is because it's full of hiking trails that weave underneath a vast canopy of trees. The paths take you past ravines, small canyons, through meadows, and deep into what seems like a never-ending forest. Wildlife indigenous to Ohio is often seen because the animals are comfortable with constant passerby, and as a result they often hang around long enough for a photo opportunity. Words do not suffice: the scenery in Penitentiary Glen is simply breathtaking.

It was beginning to rain as we pulled in the parking lot. Hurriedly we got out of the car and ran for cover under the trees. We turned our geocaching phone apps on and began to trek the three miles to ground zero. Though we were enjoying the scenery, a tense resolve hovered around us. Just as we came upon what should have been ground zero, our GPS phone app began bouncing around; we were too deep into the woods and too far away from a cell tower to receive a proper read.

Determined for success we put our phones away, went off the trail, and began to search. We upturned logs, bravely stuck our hands into tree crevices, and dug under piles of leaves. We stared at the ground while minutes passed – certain that something camouflaged would suddenly reveal itself. We got cramps in our neck staring up into the branches of the trees. We looked everywhere we could think to look, to no avail. Finally, the three of us came to rest. We stared at each other across the woods, feeling defeated, wanting to give up but unwilling to admit failure. Just then the sky opened up. The canopy of trees kept us mostly dry but the sound was almost deafening. We all looked up at the treetops welcoming the relief from the humidity and the distraction from our defeat. Then Andy looked to his right, walked over to the base of one of the most ordinary trees I've ever seen, moved a pile of leaves to the left and held up a Tupperware container. With three small words our geocaching obsession was born: "Here it is."

That was last July; since then we geocache as much as we can. Often we go as a family, but when Andy isn't with us, Andrew and I will sometimes go by ourselves. After Andy found our first cache we went on to find seven more without a single DNF. Throughout the day we updated our Facebook pages with posts and pictures tracking our progress, which drew the interest of a number of our friends. We continued to do this every time we went geocaching.

Since we were constantly fielding questions regarding what we were doing and because we were a bit fanatic ourselves, Andrew created a Facebook page we both manage called Ohio Geocachers and an Instagram hashtag (#OHGeo) we use to share pictures of our adventures. One of my photos was even shared by the official Geocaching page!

Needless to say, we no longer struggle when deciding how to spend our free time. This hobby, started on a whim, has become an addiction. But more importantly, it's something else we enjoy doing as a family; another thing that brings us happiness. We now know there's always an adventure waiting, sometimes hidden in plain view and other times ingeniously disguised. Now that we've figured out how to find it, can you blame us for becoming a bit obsessed?

How Geocaching Changed a Life

Daniel Rhodes

Lord Scoville

In the fall of 2005, I began a career working with people with developmental disabilities for one of New York State's ARCs. Working for an ARC is a very rewarding career; you get to meet a great deal of wonderful people and provide for them a family atmosphere where one may not have existed before.

It was at one of the houses that I met a young man who forever changed my life. John was an energetic young man with Asperger's and ADHD. Because of his disorders he could be challenging, especially when he became bored. Now, John had a very involved family and would often go with his father on hiking and hunting trips. On these days he would be gone for hours; when he returned home he was a bit more relaxed.

Due to John's love of the outdoors, I often found myself hiking with him on nice days. It was on one these days, while he was gathering up his notepads, camera, and whatnot, that I approached my manager and explained the idea behind geocaching. He was more than happy to let me offer up this new outdoorsy sport to John. I thanked my manager, and was off to find the person that I hoped would be my new geocaching buddy.

I found him in the garage, waiting for me to take him hiking for the day. I approached him about the idea of giving geocaching a try, and this is pretty much how the conversation went:

"John, got a question for you."

"What?" he asked, looking to the floor, probably anticipating disappointment.

"Hey, while hiking would you like to give geocaching a try?"

"What's geocaching?" he asked, lifting his head up to look at me with a curious expression.

I smiled and answered, "It's kind of a hi-tech scavenger hunt, where you use a GPS to go find a hidden container that someone else hid."

"I don't have a GPS," he said, sounding disappointed.

"It's okay. I do"

"How much money is in it?"

I laughed, then said, "Usually none, though sometimes you might find a nickel or dime. It's not that kind of cash. 'Geo' means Earth and 'Cache' means a hidden container. If it's large enough you might find dollar store items, but it's really about the adventure and the find."

"Sure, but we are still hiking, right?"

"That we are." We got into the van and off we went.

The first cache site we made it to was a bust. I found what I believed to be the spot, but no cache. I explained to John that this happens, and that you just have to call it quits sometimes and look for another one. I asked if he wanted to continue our adventure and he agreed. The next cache was just under a mile ahead and was in a hollowed-out log. I found it quickly, but thought, *If John is going to enjoy this, he should be the one to find it!*

I pretended to continue looking in different parts of the log and would say, "The GPS has me at the log, but I can't zero in on it."

Then I heard the words every cacher loves to hear, "I think I found it!" He pulled out a lock n' lock box and said, "Is this the geocache?"

"Yes it is, good job," I said. "Now let's open it and see what's inside." There was nothing much inside, just the logbook and a pen that didn't write. Luckily I had my pen with me and I let him sign the log under my geocaching name. That day we logged three finds and one DNF.

The next four weekends we found ourselves geocaching for a few hours, grabbing lunch out, and geocaching until it was time to return to the house for dinner. The funny thing about these caching adventures was that they all started with a DNF. It quickly became a joke that we should bypass the first cache on the list, because we wouldn't find it anyway. We never did bypass them, but we always said we should.

Then one day I said to my manager that I thought John would benefit from going to a geocaching event. Asperger's is a disorder under the Autism Spectrum and most people with it aren't comfortable socializing. John was no exception. I asked my manager if he would help me explain to John that an event involving people with the same interests might help him socialize. Both my manager and I were surprised when he agreed immediately; two weeks later we were attending an Easter event.

The morning of the event, we stopped by the store and picked up a breakfast pizza and a couple of sodas for the ride. Upon arrival, I introduced him to everybody as, "My friend John" and we got into the various activities of the event. It took him some time to warm up to other geocachers, but their friendliness and common interests helped to break down his wall. We hunted for some very well hidden eggs and he even won a raffle prize.

On the way back to the house, he asked me when the next event was and that he had a great time. It was wonderful to see how something as simple as geocaching and some warm faces could help this young man step outside of his comfort zone.

Since the event, John and I have attended two other events and had many great adventures. He continues to make strides to overcome his disability and wants to show others that he is not defined by his disability. Though I no longer work for the agency, I still keep in contact with him and sometimes we even geocache.

Walk With Me

Nathan Haworth

Pommiepirates

A destination, an unsolved goal

A smiley face, with footprints told.

A never ending game, you and me unfold

A secret place only you know –

For me to find and say hello

For others too, are on the case

To find that same place…

They leave a smiley face.

Finding Friends

Terri Doughty

terri and billy

We had heard about this absolutely awesome event called Geowoodstock for over a year. Before it had been too far away to attend, but this year Geowoodstock V (GCZKVX) was just a couple of states away in Raleigh, North Carolina. Though we didn't personally know anyone planning on attending, we found ourselves wrapped up in all the excitement. Registration was done and soon we were driving to an event that we couldn't even imagine.

Camping was available on the site of Geowoodstock V, even for RVs. We picked an end-site and just looked around, wide-eyed. After a bit, someone picked the site next to us. It was Ray and Emily Turner, a couple who were probably a bit older than us. They quickly made our acquaintance. Soon, we were checking out geocoins and talking about our families. Later that evening, their son, Curtis, and his family arrived.

I'm totally technology challenged and had a new GPS. Curtis had files of caches on GSAK and was more than willing to show me what to do and load what he had. Kerry was friendly and so welcoming. Before we knew it, the two campsites became one and our adventures became shared. Things even got better when the guy in the big toy hauler next to the Turners decided to put a white sheet up and showed movies for the kids!

We went from not knowing anyone to having met cachers from all over the world. At Geowoodstock V, I had donuts with a French-Canadian family and coffee with a couple from Germany. Cachers from across the country sat with us for lunch. Stories were shared and adventures explored.

From that first Geowoodstock we attended, we found more than just some caches in North Carolina. We even found more than a good time with fantastic food! We found lifelong friends who we meet up with every year. Now it feels like a big family reunion.

On a side note, the little kids that attended Geowoodstock V with Curtis and Kerry are now teenagers. With Facebook and caching, we have watched them grow up, helped with fund raisers (especially buying Girl Scout cookies), and cheered in their endeavors – even though we don't even live in the same state.

How "Penguinmolly" Became "GeopenguinsH"

Molly Houser

GeopenguinsH

While visiting us at our home in the Missouri Ozarks, my parents mentioned geocaching. I had never heard of it but they made it sound intriguing. I discovered that there were more than 40 hidden containers nearby. Some of these geocaches were even at places I frequented. How could I not know they were there? I knew then that I needed to find them all.

The first thing we needed to geocache was a GPS. I had no GPS but my parents had brought theirs. The second thing needed was a username. It was only natural that my geocaching username would be "penguinmolly." I love penguins and it was already part of my email.

"Penguins are slow and fat and they waddle," my husband said. "Do you really want your username to be associated with that?"

"Hmmmm… I'm not sure," I said. "Would you like to make yourself a sandwich for dinner and sleep on the couch tonight? He had no further comments on my username.

With the aid of my parents and their GPS, we successfully logged four geocaches during their stay. I wanted to find more but they wanted to go to Walmart. There is no Walmart where they live –imagine that! Walmart is quite an experience for them.

I was sad a few days later when the GPS was done visiting and left. I really missed that GPS a lot. Oh and I was sad my parents left, too. My geocaching adventures had come to a halt.

While my husband was supportive of my new passion for geocaching, he was not impressed with it and had no desire to participate. He did, however, promise to buy me a GPS for my birthday, which was 2 months away.

"Geocaching is something old people do!" he announced to my 29 year old self. This was not the first time he had accused me of being an old person. From my drinking of hot tea, Ginger Ale, consumption of Jell-O, and love of Werther's original candies, it was a constant phrase coming from his mouth.

I impatiently counted down the days until my birthday. I tried to find a few geocaches during this time using Google Earth but that quest turned out to be rather unsuccessful. To keep myself busy during this tortuous time of waiting I prepared my own geocaching kit. It was a backpack filled with changes of clothing, freeze dried food, MRE's, several tools, jumper cables, matches, a survival blanket, first aid kit, cash, extra shoes and a sleeping bag. My husband asked me if I preparing to go geocaching or leaving him and getting a divorce. I argued that it never hurts to be prepared.

After thinking a bit, I realized I had probably gone a little bit overboard on the geocaching kit and could take out a few items. The fact that I couldn't even lift the bag was really the deciding factor. I finally settled on a notepad, pens, trade items and trinkets, tweezers and a flashlight. I was almost ready to go!

My birthday finally arrived and with it a brand new Garmin E Trex Vista. I spun around in a few circles to calibrate the compass, uploaded the geocaches to the device, and I was off. My supportive husband was quite comfortable letting me go off on my own while he sat at home watching some sports show on television and getting chip crumbs all over the couch and floor.

I guided myself to the first geocache of the day using my new GPS. The cache was called "Somewhere in the Park". I put on my backpack and walked the 50 feet from my truck to the GZ. The GPS kept taking me near a ditch and sometimes to the middle of the road. I looked in a storm drain and found nothing.

After a while I still had not found the geocache. Why could I not find this cache? There was something I was not getting. I considered that perhaps it was the horrible username I had given myself. I told myself it was alright and I would find another one. I headed off after the second cache. I walked around in circles in the middle of a field before I gave up on that one also. I went to the third and fourth – striking out at each one.

At this point, it was starting to get dark. I had my flashlight but if I could not find these things in the daylight how would I find them in the dark? My geocaching birthday adventure had not gone as planned. I was officially the worst geocacher ever. I was also officially thirty – so double bummer. Sad and discouraged, I made the drive home.

My husband asked me how many geocaches I had found. In my sad, dejected voice I was embarrassed to proclaim that I had not found any. He was astonished at my lack of "geosense" and felt a little sorry for me, the worst geocacher in the world. He said he would go with me next time. This lifted my spirits a bit and helped slightly to dispel the sadness from that day's unsuccessful birthday geocaching trip.

Several days later we set off on our geocaching adventure together. After several successful finds my excitement for geocaching began to renew. For every cache we found I would sign the log as "penguinmolly" and "Hoss" (my husband's nickname) even though he had no actual geocaching profile and no intention to create one.

Shortly after my successful post-birthday adventure, my husband asked me when we were going geocaching again. I was thrilled! He was hooked! Geocaching soon became our weekly adventure. I officially changed the geocaching username from "Penguinmolly" to "GeopenguinsH". The "H" at the end was for the first letter of our last name. The GeopenguinsH have been happily caching together ever since!

(I would also like to note that I am no longer the worst geocacher in the world.)

Along for the Hike

Tim Martin

Rubicon Cacher

My daughter, Shelli, didn't particularly care for geocaching. Her geocaching name, Along for the Hike, pretty much sums up geocaching for her. She loved to hike and spend time enjoying the beauties of God's Creation and that's why she went on our geocaching hikes with us.

But, still, some of my best geocaching memories are with Shelli. One hike in particular comes to mind. We were hiking along a little used trail in the foothills of the Smoky Mountains in Tennessee and looking for a cache that hadn't been found for two or three years. We found it buried by nature with leaves, pine needles, and moss. I "scalped" the cache by removing a 2-3 inch toupee to get to the cache below. Of course, after we signed the log, we put the toupee back in place. Shelli enjoyed that hike as she always did and enjoyed finding the cache that hadn't been found for such a long time.

That was the last hiking and geocaching trip we took before Shelli was diagnosed, at the young age of 42, with stage 4 colon cancer. By the time she was diagnosed, the cancer had already spread to her bones, liver, and lungs.

Over the next two years and eight months, until her death, she never quit. She continued hiking and geocaching with us – even with her chemotherapy pump hanging on her waist band. She continued hiking and geocaching with us even when the chemotherapy caused severe nerve damage which caused her to lose all feeling in her feet. She would have to walk looking at her feet because she couldn't tell even where her feet were otherwise.

Another memorable geocaching trip was to the Colorado Rockies. We combined a difficult 4X4 trail with hiking and geocaching and off-roading for a great trip. This lady never quit even when she knew that the end was near. She inspired me and literally hundreds of other people including many geocachers and hikers with her fight to the end, never quit attitude, and the bright loving smile on her face even as she was dying.

Two years and eight months after the cancer was found, Shelli lost the battle on this earth and went to spend eternity in love and peace. Now, when I am on a hiking trail, it's as if I feel her presence urging me on and saying,

"Don't quit, Daddy!"

I'm sure she's hiking and geocaching in the heavens right now.

Inspiration from "The Greats"

Kelly McNeal

kegs87

Dedicated to Strider and Crowesfeat30

It was the middle of winter, and my fiancé and I were incredibly bored. After putting together about 2 dozen jigsaw puzzles, reading 9 books, and watching every movie on Netflix, we both craved the outdoors. Neither of us had any means to dress up in layers and go outside without a destination. Luckily we were introduced to geocaching.

At first we had no idea what we were doing or even if the game was real. Here we were searching a guardrail for *something* that was supposedly there. Was this a prank? Was somebody videotaping us? We reconvened, scratching our heads, and found a couple of important hints. Determined, we set out again and guess what? We found it!

We were immediately hooked on the sport. We found our 100th cache nearly two weeks later and felt comfortable about placing our own. Using some history, some humor, and a lot of creativity, we assembled a mystery cache. It was published quickly and we waited for our first find.

We waited over 24 hours. I'll admit I had a mini panic attack. I wanted to check on the cache to ensure it was okay, so we drove by the location. We pulled up and there were two cars out front. Could this be it? We both were so excited; neither of us knew what to do. So we went home and waited.

About an hour later, the email came. Hooray! It's been found! Not only that, it was found by 2 of the most recognized cachers in the area, AKA "The Greats"! They left a message giving us kudos on the cache and a favorite point. We were thrilled! It was unbelievable! I sent them an email back congratulating them on the find, and thanking them for saving my sanity. A couple days later, we got a personal invitation from those cachers to attend an event. Both my fiancé and I were nervous about meeting new people, but we did want to meet "The Greats". What the heck? Let's go!

We were able to attend and it was one of the most memorable days of my life. The place was crowded and everyone was incredibly friendly. We spent a lot of time with different groups of people and instantly connected with everyone we met. All geocachers have some crazy stories to share, and we did too. Everyone was telling stories, having fun, and nobody felt uncomfortable. Those people truly are the best bunch of people we've met. And yes, we did get to meet a few of "The Greats". It was such an honor and it gave us both more inspiration and motivation to continue geocaching.

It was sad to part ways after the event, but we've been lucky enough to bump into a few fellow cachers, including "The Greats", while we were out and about. That's what makes the sport so fun; the people who are also involved. We have made numerous friends since we've started geocaching, and I'm sure there's more to come! We probably would've never attended the event if it weren't for the personal invite. I knew it would be fun, but I didn't know limit of fun was set so high! We both are grateful to be involved with an amazing bunch of people.

Not only have we found the means to be outdoors in wintertime, but we also have reasons to spend time with Mother Nature for any day of the year! Geocaching is a good excuse to be outside, be healthy, and be happy; which was exactly the kind of motivation we needed.

Geocaching is for Lovers

Morgan Talbot

Frumious Jane

Christmas 2003 was a terrifying time for me. I'd just suffered a miscarriage that autumn, and to my shock, I was already pregnant again. I tiptoed around, afraid to sit down too hard or laugh too long, afraid it was all my fault. My weight was down to 110 pounds, concerning even for someone of my slight frame. Worries over the possibility of a second failed pregnancy darkened the Christmas season so much that I just couldn't get into the holiday spirit.

As I approached the same gestation week when my first pregnancy had failed, each day seemed to last a month. I knew if I could just get past that one milestone, my baby would be okay… and so would I.

But that week was Christmas week, and my husband, Eric, and I were traveling to my parents' house in Albany, Oregon. I was a nervous wreck. But my mother was her caring, loving self. She hadn't seen me since my miscarriage, and I had been careful not to tell anyone besides my husband that I was pregnant again, so she was full of motherly sympathy, and I managed to relax a little.

Then she brought out this little yellow tech gadget that read Magellan above the screen. "This thing gets your father out of the house," she said proudly, waggling the GPS unit at him and then at me. He grinned his snaggletooth smile from his favorite rocking chair. "I think you'd like it too," she continued. "You always did have an adventurous side."

I hadn't seen my adventurous side in a few months, but I sat rapt as she and my geeky, tech-loving father explained the basics, then the finer points, of the art of geocaching. They pulled up the geocaching.com website and pointed out the various categories of geocaches. Their icon collection was already impressive. I listened to the highlights of their new geocaching career, how they went out every day after work to nab local caches, and how my father's health was already improving with the regular exercise he got as he toted that Magellan over hill and dale.

Slowly, I sensed an idea growing in my mind. It left me full of excitement and hope—nearly foreign concepts at that point. I hadn't felt my worries recede in weeks, but my parents' new activity, along with their contagious eagerness, filled an emotional void I hadn't realized I possessed.

That night, I jotted down a poem containing seven couplets that revealed my condition—I'd been writing poetry since the age of four—and in the morning, I nabbed that Magellan GPS unit before my parents got up.

Outside in the drizzle, wearing my husband's jacket and my mom's rubber-soled outdoor slippers, I took coordinate readings in seven spots on my parents' century-old property. Then I tooled back inside and dug out my parents' film-canister collection. Within half an hour, I'd constructed and hidden my first multi-cache and was waiting eagerly for my parents to wake up.

Gone were my dark clouds of fear and worry. Though it was raining outside, I swore I could feel the sun on my face. For the first time in far too long, my heart had gotten its bearings.

Breakfast seemed to last for a few years, but eventually my parents fired up the Magellan and plugged in my first set of coordinates. I trailed them around the soggy yard as they waved the yellow device around, nailing down coordinate sets and rummaging through their dripping shrubbery with eager hands. All the while, they kept up a running commentary about what I was up to and what the rhyming couplets they pulled from each film canister could be hinting at.

Finally, they reached the last container and read the end of the poem. Learning I was pregnant again, my mother threw her arms around me and squeezed me tight. In her comforting embrace, I settled into the belief that everything would truly be okay.

My husband and I took up geocaching. My daughter was born the following August. I invited my BFF to geocache with me, and we and our toddlers toured all over town, hitting every playground geocache within twenty miles. My daughter and I traveled with my husband for his work and cached our way through several West Coast cities. I cached during my next pregnancy until I couldn't bear to walk, and then I virtually explored the world by reading Earth Cache webpages. We took our baby son out while teaching our daughter how to hunt for caches. I started writing again, as I had back in college, and one day it struck me how perfectly the principles of geocaching fit with the necessary curiosity a mystery sleuth requires. I wrote a geocaching mystery novel, then another, and another. An industry connection led me to a small press who accepted my Caching Out series for publication. Now geocachers around the world read my caching books and share my love/hate relationship with the unsolved.

Geocaching is for lovers—lovers of exploration, curiosity, adventure, and fun. Geocaching is for lovers of friendship and family, for lovers of the outdoors, and for sweetheart lovers. Geocaching embraces those who are unafraid of the future and unfettered by the past. Geocaching set me free from my fears and gave me a path to finding myself. I will be forever grateful to my parents and to geocaching for giving me a way out of that darkest of places just when I needed it.

Extras

Common Geocaching Terms

Archive – Archiving a cache removes the listing from public view on Geocaching.com. This action is usually taken when a cache owner does not intend to replace a cache after it has been removed. As an alternative to archiving, the cache owner can temporarily disable their cache if they plan to provide maintenance on the cache or replace the container within one month.

Attribute – These are icons on a cache detail intended to provide helpful information to geocachers who wish to find specific types of caches. These icons represent unique cache characteristics, including size, whether the cache is kid friendly, if it is available 24 hours a day, if you need special equipment and more. Attributes are also a tool to help you filter the types of caches you would like to search for when building a Pocket Query (see Pocket Query).

Benchmark – Using your GPS unit and/or written directions provided by NOAA's National Geodetic Survey (NGS), you can seek out NGS survey markers and other items that have been marked in the USA.

Bookmark List – A Premium Member feature that can be used to group cache listings in whatever way you like. You may want a bookmark list of caches you intend to find this weekend, or perhaps an "all-time favorite" list you can share with friends.

Cache – A shortened version of the word geocache. (See Geocache).

Cacher – One who participates in geocaching. Also known as geocacher.

Caches Along a Road – A road that has caches at every available pull-off, or nearly every pull-off. These are popular for people who like Park and Grab caches.

Caches along a Route – A Premium Member feature that allows you to identify caches along a specific route for quick and easy geocaching. You can choose from routes already created by other geocachers or use Google Earth to build your own unique trip.

Caches along a Trail – This means that there are multiple caches placed along a hiking trail. Similar to Caches along a Road, Caches along a Trail is an "easy" way to find a lot of caches in a short amount of time.

Datum – A datum is something used as a basis for calculating and measuring. In the case of GPS, datums are different calculations for determining longitude and latitude for a given location. Currently, Geocaching uses the WGS84 datum.

Dipping – The act of logging a Travel Bug or Geocoin into a cache, and immediately logging it back into ones possession. Someone cachers "dip" a Travel Bug or Geocoin in order to register miles traveled before placing the trackable for someone else to find. Some people use a "personal traveler" to track their miles between caches, and will "dip" the traveler into each cache they find.

Drunken Bee Dance – The movements of a geocacher, trying to pinpoint Ground Zero, chasing the directional arrow first one direction and then another, has been termed the Drunken Bee Dance.

EarthCache – This is one of several unique cache types. An EarthCache is a cache that promotes geoscience education. Visitors to EarthCaches can see how our planet has been shaped by geological processes, how we manage the resources and how scientists gather evidence to learn about the Earth.

Event Cache – This is one of several unique cache types. Events are gatherings set up by local geocachers and geocaching organizations to meet players and to discuss geocaching.

GC Code – A unique identifier associated with every geocache listing. The GC Code starts with the letters "GC" and is followed by other alphanumeric characters.

GeoArt – A series of caches placed to form a shape. Example include hearts, a person, animal, etc. Caches may or may not be multi-stages caches.

Geocache – A hidden container that includes a logbook for geocachers to sign. A geocache may also include trade items.

Geocoin – Geocoins work similarly to Groundspeak Travel Bugs® (see

Travel Bugs) in that they are trackable and can travel the world, picking up stories from geocache to geocache. Geocoins are often created as signature items by geocachers and can also be used as collectibles.

Geomuggle – see Muggle.

Groundspeak – The parent corporation for geocaching.com. Groundspeak also manages waymarking.com and wherigo.com

Groudspeak Lackey – A "Groundspeak Lackey" is a term used to refer to the employees and founders of Groundspeak who do the most basic tasks to support the overall needs of the community. This willingness to serve each other and provide recreation for a worldwide community is a core value of our company.

Ground Zero – The location at which the GPS unit is saying the geocache container is located. Also known as GZ.

Hitchhiker – A hitchhiker is an item that is placed in a cache, and has instructions to travel to other caches. Sometimes they have logbooks attached so you can log their travels. All trackable items can also be called a hitchhiker.

Latitude – Latitude and longitude create a waypoint. Latitude is the angular distance north or south from the earth's equator measured through 90 degrees.

Letterbox – A letterbox or letterboxing is similar to Geocaching, but you use a series of clues to find a container. Once you find the container (or letterbox), you use the carved stamp from the box, stamp your personal logbook and return that stamp to the letterbox. You then use your carved stamp and stamp the letterbox's logbook.

Longitude – Latitude and longitude create a waypoint. Longitude is the angular distance measured on a great circle of reference from the intersection of the adopted zero meridian with this reference circle to the similar intersection of the meridian passing through the object.

Mega-Event Cache – This is one of several cache types. A Mega-Event cache is similar to an Event Cache but it is much larger. Among other considerations, a Mega-event cache must be attended by 500+ people. Typically, Mega Events are annual events and attract geocachers from all over the world.

Muggle – A non-geocacher. Based on "Muggle" from the Harry Potter series, which is a non-magical person.

Muggled – The discovery of a cache by a non-geocacher. Also can be termed "geomuggled". When someone refers to a cache as having been muggled, it almost always means the cache was stolen or vandalized.

Multi-Cache – This is one of several cache types. A multi-cache, or multiple cache, involves two or more locations, the final location being a physical container. There are many variations, but most multi-caches have a hint to find the second cache, and the second cache has hints to the third, and so on.

Mystery or Puzzle Caches – This is one of several cache types. The "catch-all" of cache types, this form of cache can involve complicated puzzles you will first need to solve to determine the coordinates. Examples include complicated ciphers, simple substitutions, arithmetical quizzes and clues cleverly hidden within the graphics.

NAD27 – Stands for North American Datum 1927. The precursor to WGS84. Many maps still use the NAD27 datum , so always check before using a GPS unit with a map.

Nano – An unofficial cache size. A nano cache is usually considerably smaller than the typical micro. One popular container is approximately the size of an eraser on the end of a pencil.

Officer McFriendly – Term for an encounter with any law enforcement officer while out geocaching.

Personal Traveler – A trackable item that is activated but is not released. The owner of the item dips it in caches but it never leaves the owner's possession.

Pocket Query – (PQ) A Premium Member feature, a Pocket Query is custom geocache search that you can have emailed to you on a daily or weekly basis. Pocket Queries give you the ability to filter your searches so you only receive information on the caches you want to search for.

Reviewer – World-wide network of volunteers who publish the geocache after the listing is submitted to geocaching.com.

ROT13 – Hints for geocaches are encrypted using a simple format where each of the letters are rotated 13 characters up or down in the alphabet.

Signal – Signal is the official mascot of geocaching.com. Designed by artist Koko, Signal is a frog with an GPS antenna on its head.

Signature Item – An item unique to a specific geocacher that is left behind in caches to signify that they visited that cache. These often include personal geocoins, tokens, pins, craft items or calling cards. These are acceptable trade items and may be removed from a cache.

Spoiler – A spoiler is information gives details that can lead the next cacher to the cache. It is like an accidental hint. An example would be a post for a geocache like: "We parked right next to the log where the cache was hidden."

Swag – Are the items that are left in a geocache for trade. Ths is sometimes expressed as the acronym 'Stuff We All Get" however the word "swag" is not really an acronym.

Trackable Item – Any item that can be tracked on geocaching.com.

Trade Item – Items in a geocache that are available to be taken. It is a best practice that you leave an item of equal or greater value for each item you take.

Traditional Cache – The original cache type consisting of at least a container and a logbook. The coordinates listed on the traditional cache page are the exact location for the cache.

Travel Bug Hotel – A geocache with the intended purpose of acting as an exchange point for Travel Bugs. These are almost always regular or larger sized containers.

Travel Bug® – A Groundspeak Travel Bug is a trackable tag that you attach to an item. This allows you to track your item on Geocaching.com. The item becomes a hitchhiker that is carried from cache to cache (or person to person) in the real world and you can follow its progress online.

Waypoint - A waypoint is a reference point for a physical location on Earth. Waypoints are defined by a set of coordinates that typically include longitude, latitude and sometimes altitude. Every geocache listed on our website is a waypoint. Geocaching.com generates a unique "GC Code" associated with every geocache listing.

Getting Started Geocaching

If you're reading this book as a muggle, I hope you'll consider joining us in this wonderful family-friendly game! You'll need a few items to get started:

- **GPS** – you can get a good starter unit for around $100! You really don't need anything fancy.

- **GPS App for your phone** – this has limited accuracy in the "wild" areas of the world where you're away from cell towers. The app is free and it's a great way to get started.

- **Geocaching account** – visit Geocaching.com to join. Accounts are free or you can upgrade to a premium membership and access additional features.

And really, that's it! From there, you can search for geocaches near you. Some handy things to bring with you on your adventure are:

- A pen
- Small trinkets for swag
- A "poking stick" (as Andrea Tantillo calls it)

As you're getting started on your adventures, remember that you have to develop your "geosense" which allows you to guess where a cache might be. If you can go out with a cacher who has a few finds, that's a great way to get started and have some successes.

Please keep your common sense! Take water and snacks, tell somebody where you're going, and don't stick your fingers into strange holes – there might be a critter in there! Like any outdoor adventure, geocaching has its risks so please stay safe.

All of geocaching really relies on the honor system: you'll re-hide the cache as good or better than you found it, you will clean up after yourself (and take out "extra" trash), you'll only claim finds you actually locate, and your trade items are quality.

For more information, and to create your geocaching membership account, go to www.Geocaching.com

Printed in Great Britain
by Amazon

32464666R00072